55.⁰⁰

VISUAL ANALOGY

The MIT Press   Cambridge, Massachusetts   London, England

VISUAL ANALOGY

CONSCIOUSNESS AS
THE ART OF CONNECTING

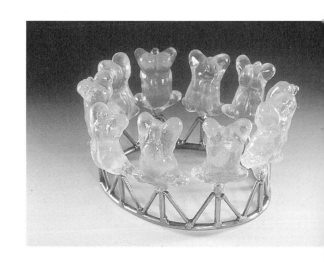

Barbara Maria Stafford

"Not Disjointive" by Mary Gray Hughes appeared in *American Literary Review* 1, no. 2 (Fall 1990), and is reprinted by permission of the author and the American Literary Review.

This book was set in Janson by Graphic Composition, Inc. and was printed and bound in the United States of America.

Library of Congress Cataloging-in-Publication Data

Stafford, Barbara Maria, 1941–
    Visual analogy : consciousness as the art of connecting / Barbara Maria Stafford.
      p. cm.
    Includes bibliographical references and index.
    ISBN 0-262-19421-X (alk. paper)
    1. Analogy.   2. Consciousness.
  BD190.S78   1999
    169—dc21   99-15240
                                                                      CIP

Contents

Poem Dedicatory

Not Disjointive
Mary Gray Hughes

For death
is not
disjointive
but a need
the body
owes
the earth,
an end
to the
presumption
that this
space
is mine
through
time,
a
reconciliation
with
those shapes
which will be
made
from molecules
once mine.

List of Illustrations

Preface

In the autumn of 1997, I presented the Page-Barbour Lectures at the University of Virginia in Charlottesville. It was the most difficult, exhilarating, and challenging project I had ever embarked upon. The charge was to speak on virgin material: nothing was to have appeared in print before. I was to give three scholarly lectures during the space of a single week on a major topic of my choice, one that would address the entire university community and an enlightened general public to boot. In addition, I was to hold informal discussions with interested faculty and students coming from art history, political theory, literature, philosophy, and religious studies programs, and professional schools such as the Law School and the Thomas Jefferson School of Government. At the end, I was to deliver a publishable manuscript.

In preparing these talks, I decided I would write them not as hourlong speeches but as short colloquial essays on intertwined themes. My aim was to recuperate the ancient and intrinsically visual *method* of analogy for modern times. Foucault has been dead for over a decade. I thought it time to develop a sophisticated theory and practice of resemblance rather than continuing endlessly to subdivide distinctions. I also believed the moment ripe to look at the rich and varied imaging or figurative tradition, rather than linguistics, for a connective model of visual rhetoric adequate to our networked, multimedia future.

Brief as they are, these essays also form part of a long-term project of mine to put art history (or imaging, as I prefer) at the center of the major intellectual issues of our times. *Body Criticism* located the new medical imaging technologies of transparency within the larger ambit of early modern representational strategies. *Artful Science* addressed the rhetoric of corruption swirling around infotainment and suggested that, learning from the past, we could reinvent a delightful, sensory-based education. *Good Looking* wrestled with the digital revolution and proposed an aesthetical ethics for the Internet. With *Visual Analogy*, I want to place imaging and imagists in the middle of the philosophical, neurobiological, and cognitive science debates surrounding the nature of consciousness.

The origin of this book precludes any claims to comprehensiveness. Instead, I think of the following four chapters as depth charges roiling the ocean of predication, parting the waters to reveal flashes of bridging processes by which one can persuasively show that something is *like* something else or *participates* in what it is not—whether another human being, or an alien culture, or a strange environment, or a technological device of our manufacture, or a subtle state of mind, or one of the infinite particulars of the organic and inorganic universe. Although it would take a lifetime to construct an exhaustive history of analogy, I have nonetheless tried to bring to this brief study some chronological sweep, a compelling range of issues, and a relational analysis of art and nonart objects, to demonstrate the dire need—in all fields and disciplines—for ways of seeing sameness-in-difference. Indeed, it is impossible to have a sophisticated theory of difference without an equally nuanced conception of similarity.

I am deeply honored and grateful to the Page-Barbour Committee, especially Daniel Ehnboim and Allen Megill, for having extended this invitation and permitting me to stretch my wings. I also thank the members of the University of Chicago graduate seminar on visual analogy, which I taught as a "dry run" during that same fall term, for their willingness to venture beyond the academic borders of deconstructionism and poststructuralism. But, above all, I valued their good-natured skepticism and hard questions, which kept pushing me to clarify meaning. This dynamic group included Arnold Bosse, Christopher Collins, Robert Donnelly, Alison Gamble, Stacy Hand, Kristina Mucinskas, Mario Pereira, Elizabeth Patterson, Matthew Percy, Jamee Rosa, David Snyder, and Robert Wyrod. Many, I am proud to say, are now embarked on path-breaking theses, ranging from Vico's analogical theory of the imagination to the educational impact of Nintendo's Super Mario video games, which make the child identical with the controlling computer.

Without a blissful year as a Getty Scholar in 1994–1995 (I was a lucky participant in the last "class" at Santa Monica before the momentous move up the magic mountain above Brentwood), I would have had nothing to say at all. I am eternally thankful to Salvatore Settis for issuing the call to ride west. I also owe a special debt to Frances Terpak, Curator of Special Collections at the Getty Research Institute, for her unflagging optimism, expert sleuthing, and sheer persistence. (We are collaborating on an exhibition on vanished technology for the year 2001, which is intimately connected to the subject of this book.) I am also grateful to Karl

Clausberg and two anonymous reviewers for their helpful comments on the manuscript.

Finally, there are no words adequate to express the warm support, friendly encouragement, and nurture of the soul provided by the authors' circle, the *femmes savantes*. They gave me the rarest gift of all by offering a space where writers were encouraged to disarm themselves, to listen to one another with attention and care, allowing each voice to speak from its individual center. Sally Chappell, our muse, Florence Cohen, Mary Gray Hughes, Wadad Kadi, Joan Perkin, Ingrid Rowland, Tilde Sankevitch: where would I have been without you? I toast those luminous lunches, lingering into the late afternoon, which helped dispel the loneliness of the long-distance author. This book is respectfully dedicated to these beautiful, courageous, and accomplished women.

Preview: The Game
of Back and Forth

In his witty essay on "Flirtation," Georg Simmel spars with Plato about the to and fro of love. It is, according to the ancient philosopher, an intermediate state between having and not-having. Although this definition, with its invocation of a rhythmic rocking between two poles, proves far from satisfactory to the modern critic of commodity culture, it begins to get at the subject of this brief book. Analogy, born of the human desire to achieve union with that which one does not possess, is also a passionate process marked by fluid oscillations. Perceiving the lack of something—whether physical, emotional, spiritual, or intellectual—inspires us to search for an approximating resemblance to fill its place. That theological, philosophical, rhetorical, and aesthetic quest gave birth to the middle term: the delayed not-yet or the allusive not-quite. This fleeting entity—participating both in what one has and what one has not, like and unlike the yearned-for experience—temporarily allows the beholder to feel near, even interpenetrated by, what is distant, unfamiliar, different. Denial and accommodation, retreat and advance, absence and presence—just like the teasing interplay of the flirt's alternating tactics—mark the *capriccio* dynamics of analogy's jumps from antithesis to synthesis and then back again.

One meaning of analogy goes back to Greek mathematics, where it referred to proportion or the due ratio among numbers in a set. This rational sense was extended by Aristotle, among others, to embrace non-mathematical relations in areas like justice, virtue, poetics. By means of a disciplined inferential logic, one might establish measurable connections between incongruent phenomena through a stepped system of predication. The essence of the Parmenidean One, for example, could be hypothesized by abstracting from the excellences of the many that descended from it as first cause and could then be reattributed, in purified numerical form, to their superior source.

But there is still another meaning of analogy, less studied and not easy to keep separate from the proportional kind. I identify this qualitative theory of participation specifically with Plato. The subsequent mixups occurring between these two techniques led, I suggest, to the theurgic be-fuddlements of the later Neoplatonists and Christian Gnostics who were responsible for collapsing analogy into mystical incoherence. Importantly, while the method based on establishing quantitative proportions drew on a geometrical language of equality and inequality, that grounded in the rhet-oric of participation employed the mimetic vocabulary of similarity and dissimilarity. I argue that these were important distinctions with real conceptual consequences that have not been properly attended to. What had been considered a provisional equilibrium among divergent integers or a coquettish vacillation between veiling and unveiling appearances either hardened into a formulaic dualism or vanished within a lengthening scale of symbols.

The truncated story I tell has two main theses. First, I propose that both the proportional and the participatory varieties of analogy are inherently visual. It requires perspicacity to see what kinds of adjustments need to be made between uneven cases to achieve a tentative harmony. It also presupposes discernment to discover the relevant likeness in unlike things. To the best of my knowledge, the optical necessity driving the entire system has not been pointed out before in the analyses devoted to this venerable conundrum. This brings me to the additional, novel claim that the visual arts are singularly suited to provide explanatory power for the nature and function of the analogical procedure. Second, I propose that at certain key moments in the past, and irrevocably with the Jena romantics at the turn of the nineteenth century, analogy as a reciprocating method and mentality was overturned by *disanalogy*. I call this massive cultural implosion into insurmountable and unrepresentable contradiction—separated by uncommunicative emptiness or clogged with conflicting distinctions—*allegory*, to indicate its literary origins within a negative hermeneutics. It is as if the two throbbing poles of Simmel's flirtation, perpetually pulsing the disclosure and concealment of self, sedimented into parallel geological strata stretching to infinity or fractured into countless shards. The homogeneous aloofness of cult initiates and gated communities addressing only themselves contributes to a mosaic society in which arguing groups exclusively seek to promote their own separate interests.

The pages that follow attempt to flesh out these claims. The main thrust of the opening chapter is to expose the vacancy of our current disciplinary and social landscape, voided of anything standing tangibly in between oppositional choices for conduct and simultaneously glutted, choked by innumerable competing esoteric differences. Chapter 2 is concerned with the analogy/allegory polemics. Insofar as these are continually played off against each other, they possess different looks or styles that weave or fragment human experience. Chapter 3 describes how the intuitive attraction between lovers provided, early on, the genealogical or genetic prototype for analogical relationships of all sorts. From the pre-Socratics to Leibniz, a system of captivating forces abstractly mirrored the dynamics of sexual bonding. The universe possessed order and beauty because of the parentage of the four elements. Even with all their dissimilarities, kinships among these material components might be recognized and correlated. By analogical extension, this physical intercourse gave rise to evolving families of associated ideas or developing mental categories. To inference is to pair explicit with implicit properties of objects and so to collect them into new ensembles. Chapter 4 gets to one of the great puzzles of the late twentieth century: What is the appropriate relationship between the biological and social sciences and the humanities? Here I put the specifically visual aspects of analogy to work on cognitivism. The structure of human consciousness is at the center of fierce and fascinating disputes. But the definition of self-awareness mustered by the proponents of the new philosophy of mind is impoverished, I argue, because it does not include the rich connective evidence provided by the humanistic visual arts.

I have written this meditation on relation for an audience as broad as those students, faculty, and others from outside the circle of academia who attended my lectures. Since the format is compressed and the subject is multidisciplinary, I have supported my arguments with extensive footnotes for the experts. I do not believe, however, that they are necessary for the interested nonspecialist. If, on occasion, the path taken seems maddeningly neither straight nor uniform, neither is the wandering topic. Nonetheless, I hope in some small way to have restored analogy and perception to the forefront of some of the major issues confronting our times. One of the most central of these is the need to revisualize how we create attachments.

1

Postmodernism
and the Annihilation
of Resemblance

And simulation is still not duplication.
John Searle, "I Married a Computer"

Why analogy? Today even the name sounds anachronistic, if not down-right delusional, conjuring up fantasies of the free-associationist impulse run amok. Umberto Eco recently ridiculed it as "Hermetic semiosis," the cabbalistic obsession and paranoid credulity that uncritically leaps to link everything in the cosmos to everything else.[1] Yet Plato, inspired by the early Ionian school, declared that analogy was "the most beautiful bond possible."[2]

Analogia, or *ana/logos*, signifies "according to due ratio" and "according to the same kind of way."[3] *Analogon*, then, is the proportion or similarity that exists between two or more apparently dissimilar things: like the ten-sile harmony that Parmenides maintained fitted together fire and earth, or Empedocles believed conjoined love and hate, or Anaxagoras thought tied the visible to the invisible realm. Both ancient and modern, its figures of reconciliation expressed how self could relate to others, how human beings might exist in reciprocity with society or in harmony with nature.

With Plato, Aristotle, the Neoplatonists, Aquinas, Kant, Mill, Nietz-sche, Heidegger, and the late Wittgenstein, this elastic knot of unity as-sumed a wider epistemological meaning than numerical equidistance and logical symmetry. It emerged as a form of dialectics attempting to bridge the seen and the unseen, the known and the unknown. Proportionality, or the like and reciprocal relation between two proportions, is distinct from mere identity, the illusion of full adequacy in the explication of one term by means of another.

I want to recuperate analogy, then, as a general theory of artful inven-tion and as a practice of intermedia communication. Knowledge is a heu-retic system[4] always in pursuit of equivalences for one thing or another. It results when abstractions are made concrete, when family ties between dis-tant or separated events are exposed. In this chapter, I hope to do three things. I want, first, to provide a brief overview of the historical attitude toward analogy, one that counters Eco's deprecatory interpretation. Sec-ond, I want to show how analogy as the webworking strategy par excel-lence became almost exclusively linked with its wrong turnings. And third, I want to consider the dire need for analogical applications in the contem-porary world. By raising a periscope, so to speak, over the social, biological, technological, and disciplinary landscape, I shall argue that we need both to retrieve and to construct a more nuanced picture of resemblance and connectedness.

Most fundamentally, analogy is the vision of ordered relationships articulated as similarity-in-difference. This order is neither facilely affirmative nor purchased at the expense of variety. Analogues retain their individual intensity while being focused, interpreted, and related to other distinctive analogues and the prime analogue.[5] We should imagine analogy, then, as a participatory performance, a ballet of centripetal and centrifugal forces lifting gobbets of sameness from one level or sphere to another. Analogy correlates originality with continuity, what comes after with what went before, ensuing parts with evolving whole. This transport of predicates involves a mutual sharing in, or partaking of, certain determinable quantitative and qualitative attributes through a mediating image.

As Vico suggested in the *New Science* (1725, 1730, 1744), with his concept of the *verum factum*, we can never completely know nature because God created it. Society and history, on the other hand, were shaped by human beings. We can begin to understand these man-made creations by inventively seeking correspondences between early myths, religious rites, political institutions, pictographic languages and those of our own day. *Fantasia* permits the mind to connect disparate things in analogical form. Like the crisscross, in Wittgenstein's *Philosophical Investigations* (1945), cross-cultural knowledge demands imaginative jumps through space and time to discover continuities and discontinuities with current events. The leap of the *ingenium* captures this intersecting process for going on, for continually approaching the same points afresh from different directions and vantages.[6]

As we shall see in later chapters, conceiving analogy as the subsumption of two inferior, dichotomous terms into a superior, third one (as in Hegel's principle of *Aufhebung* or Marx's theory of exchange) is an elision that dangerously veers into the monism of allegory. In contrast, seeing analogy as analogy, that is, as a metamorphic and metaphoric practice for weaving discordant particulars into a partial concordance, spurs the imagination to discover similarities in dissimilarities (as in Leibniz's *ars combinatoria*).

Whether interpreted negatively as collapsing separate categories or, positively, as associating apparent incompatibilities, the goal of analogy must sound either poignant or wrong-headed to late twentieth-century ears. The hallmark of contemporary experience is an absence of in-betweenness. No third thing mediates between the immediacy of the current event and its antecedent. Analogy's tireless hunt after a common concept ensured, by contrast, that no two opinions were ever perfectly alike, nor were they ever completely foreign to one another. Nothing was permitted to remain locked within its autonomous denotation, to languish within an isolating frame of reference. Today, however, we possess no language for talking about resemblance, only an exaggerated awareness of difference. In light of the current fragmentation of social discourse, the inability to reach out and build a consensus on anything that matters, analogy's double avoidance of self-sameness and total estrangement again seems pertinent. Our planet is staggering under an explosion of discontinuous happenings exhibited as if they had no historical precedents. We are overloaded with personal statements, irreducibly distinctive subjects, and contradictory opinions.[7]

We live in an age of otherness, of assertive identities, of the "diversification of diversity,"[8] and have been doing so since the eruption of romantic individualism during the late eighteenth century. The gloomy monster in Mary Shelley's *Frankenstein* (1818) embodies just such exaggerated singularity. One of the lessons of the novel is that a wholly original creature, an autonomous thing without precedent, is doomed to the loneliness of absolute freedom without ties. Recall that his basic problem was the fact that he could not find his match,[9] or even someone *like* him—whether father, mother, or wife. Being so intractably unique, without filiation, he is quite literally impossible to analogize or bring into familial relationship with the genealogical structure of the universe. This laboratory-induced grotesque lived in enforced juxtaposition with strangers. Such alienation proved prophetic. At the close of the twentieth century, the erosion of communal life and the multiplication of bizarre cults encouraging the simultaneous withdrawal into mindless acquiescence and embrace of dissident idiosyncrasy has left us equally incapable of speaking across differences.

Analogy—the art of sympathetic thought thriving in antiquity and cresting at the close of the baroque era—forged bonds between two or more incongruities and spanned incommensurables. Like the magnificently frescoed (by Daniel Gran) papyrus-, manuscript-, map-, music score-, and book-lined interior of the *Prunksaal* of the Austrian National

Library (founded in 1526 and housed since 1727 in a baroque wing of the old Imperial Palace in Vienna), knowledge is both a collection and a labyrinth. Paintings of more modest private holdings also show that early modern polymaths had no illusions about universal comprehensiveness (fig. 1).[10] No repository—whether big or small—can contain all learning, not even a digital database. Since no form of organization, no matter how encyclopedic, can give complete access to the diversity of existing or imagined things, analogy provides opportunities to travel back into history, to spring forward in time, to leap across continents. This was never more true than in today's global informatics reeling under the exponential explosion of publications, the hyperspecialized segmentation of areas, and the intransigence of warring methodologies.[11]

Searching for crisscrossing elements to yoke microcosm with macrocosm demanded energy and discernment in the beholder (fig. 2). A performative rhetoric spun a vast web of attracting and repelling forces, chained together by correspondences, linking the lunar to the sublunar world. Homeopathic magic, compelling like to be influenced by like, goes back to Babylonian astrological divination. Priestly prognosticators scanned the heavens looking for auspicious or inauspicious signs concerning the fate of kings, nations, and crops, the outcome of political events and military campaigns.[12] The earth and sky were literally "ominous," emitting signals in the form of portents, compiled and inscribed on tablets as early as 2000 B.C. This "physiognomic" understanding of nature, based on the active perception and construction of affinities, was periodically overthrown—starting already in late antiquity—by a negative allegoresis composed of irreconcilable antinomies. One can think, more recently, of how the structuralist vogue for investigating homologies was discarded by Foucault who insisted, instead, on rupture and dissonance. Central to Lévi-Strauss's anthropology had been the burning question of whether, in a mythology quite unconnected to European antiquity, one could not find the same elements in the same combination.[13]

During the early modern period, specifically, the Leibnizian polyphonic play of the world—visualizable as a magnificent, radiating-aisled baroque palace or church whose multiple distinct paths converged at the center (fig. 3)—hardened into a dualistic poetics and a fracturing aesthetics. Contradictory and ironic structures govern the writings of Novalis, Coleridge, Baudelaire, and Nietzsche.[14] All are gloomily obsessed by vi-

1. Jan van der Heyden, *Library Interior with Still Life,* 1711–1712.

2. Athanasius Kircher, frontispiece to *Ars Magna
Lucis et Umbrae,* 1671.

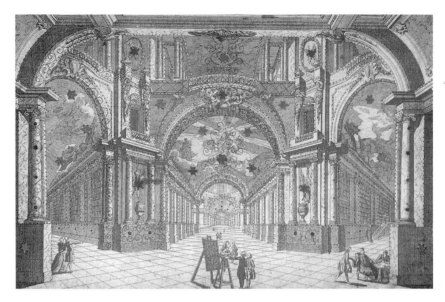

3. Anonymous, *Vue d'optique of a Baroque Interior*, late 18th century.

sions of an unattainable whole and a universe in tatters. It is not by chance that Derrida's deconstructionism further mined the chasm between the Ideal and the real already dug by the Jena romantics.[15] According to Schelling, every person is driven by nature to seek the Absolute, but as soon as human reason tries to grasp it, it disappears. This intuitive vision of perfection "drifts above him always, but it is, as Fichte excellently expressed it, only there, insofar as one does *not* possess it, and as soon as one seizes it, it vanishes." All description, therefore, is "merely negative and never brings forth the Absolute itself, making it present to the soul in its true essence."[16]

Instead of the fluidities of compossibility, contradictions atomistically pushed apart the corporeal and intelligible realms. Conceiving existence as a lesson in absolute contrariety is exemplified in the oppositional structure determining Joseph Wright of Derby's confrontational *Old Man and Death* (fig. 4). Romantic logic—erected on a paradoxical play of binaries rather than on a dialectics of reconciliation—tended to disintegrate around its two skeptical axes. Members of this post–French Revolutionary generation were the descendants of those Ramist, Cartesian, and Calvinist contrarians

4. Joseph Wright of Derby, *The Old Man and Death,* 1773.

of the Protestant seventeenth century no longer able or willing to coordinate competing religious perspectives. Like the Milton of *Paradise Lost,*[17] they were acutely aware of inhabiting a ruined realm in which the Renaissance possibility of magically mirroring the cosmos in words and images had shattered.

The romantic ideal of mental juggling, urging that one hold critical judgments in perpetual equilibrium, all too frequently descended into contradiction, bringing bitterness, pessimism, and ultimately nihilism in its wake. Even Friedrich Schlegel's adoption of the "both and" stance typical of Socratic *eironeia,*[18] rather than rhetorical irony which has as its definition saying one thing and meaning another, fails, in the end, to escape the negative-destructive pole of the desired synthesis of antitheses. In his *Lyceum* fragments of 1797 and *Athenaeum* fragments of 1798, the act of simultaneously combining mutually exclusive ideas or incongruous states-

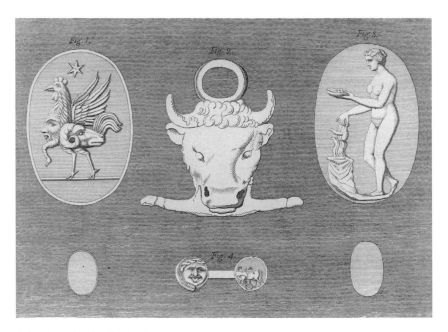

5. Richard Payne Knight, *The "Symbolical Language" of the Ancients,* 1786.

of-mind hinged not on resolving the conflict between them but on preserving their individual autonomy. Like the monstrous grotesques incised on the cameos and intaglio gems fascinating late eighteenth-century antiquarians, dichotomies were raised into an ironic—that is, a disingenuous—synthesis, one that merely appeared to destroy contrasts (fig. 5).

This illusory coalescence ultimately tainted the work of art, turning it into an allegory whose cold, contrived exterior gnawed away at its imaginative, but fictitious, interior. "Every sentence, every book that does not contradict itself is imperfect," Schlegel declared.[19] From Velásquez's over-the-hill soldier tricked out in a scarlet mantle and the gleaming but ill-fitting helmet of Mars (fig. 6) to Manet's model Victorine Meurand uncomfortably suited in the tight costume of a Spanish espada (fig. 7), the slippage between mask and wearer became increasingly marked.

In the novella *Elective Affinities* (1809), Goethe brilliantly exposed and critiqued the negative dialectics undergirding Novalis's *Naturphilosophie.*

6.   Diego Velásquez da Silva, *The God Mars,*
         1640–1642.

7. Edouard Manet, *Mademoiselle Victorine in the Costume of an Espada*, 1862.

Stretching Robert Hooke's notion of the "sociability" existing between the opposite poles of a magnet,[20] Goethe created a scientific romance to meditate on the mysteries of why and how people are drawn toward one another. He also expanded Newton's theory of gravitational attraction to include chemical and electrical phenomena, correlating these with the lodestone-and-iron-filing patterns of human behavior. Inspired by the fact that mixing certain chemical compounds resulted in their astonishing exchange of "partners," Goethe developed an extended material metaphor to capture the emotional switches occurring among a quartet of lovers. The Captain, one of the story's four characters, thus explained how close and strong, remote and weak connections—just as in an experimentally induced precipitation—really became interesting "only when they bring about separations." The chemist, then, was primarily an "artist in separating." To which the horrified Charlotte vainly protested: "Uniting is a greater and more deserving art."[21]

Paradoxically, the paramount romantic virtue of sympathy was the opposite of analogy. Goethe's novel used the artificially stimulated breakup of elements, violently severed in a chemistry laboratory, to capture the Jena romantics' glorification of the chaotic fragment.[22] In the process, he revealed the allegorical underpinnings of this group's conviction that any "friendship" between ruptured parts—whether nonhuman or human—was ultimately unrepresentable. Romanticism's essentially nonvisual, dissective procedure expressed the isolation, intense interdependence, and resulting disconnectedness from the rest of creation felt by two things or discrete individuals joined in a tenuously exclusive union.[23]

After the polymathic epoch of wonders and curiosities was decisively cast off by Cartesian systematizers, Hobbesian skeptics, and romantic ironists, the inductive art of finding and making connections became aligned, as I suggested, with its hermeneutical excesses. It also suffered by being exclusively associated with its occult manifestations. Even more basically, analogy's mimetic impulse to couple unlike presentations was taken by Stoic-inspired critics as proof of its deceptive illusionism. The deist high Enlighteners, especially, identified a blurring and conflating analogy with astrological necromancy, with the pagan demonology of Neoplatonic "charlatans" past and present (fig. 8), with "Greek Cabbalists," "miracle-mongering" sophists, and polytheistic sects of every stripe.[24] Among these syncretizing "Enthusiasts"—attempting to integrate the cults of Egypt,

8. Karl von Eckartshausen, *Female Apparition*
Appearing to Two Men, 1788–1791.

Syria, and the entire Greco-Roman world—were the number-rigging Pythagoreans, the Egyptian adepts Apollonius of Tyana and Proclus, and the dream analysts Macrobius, Lucian, and Apuleius. All set store by animism, possession, inspiration, and the craft of inducing out-of-body experiences.[25] There is an uncanny parallelism between Second Sophistic[26] philosophical debates, occurring during the later second and third centuries in Rome, and eighteenth-century ethical invectives directed against an eclectic, uncritical mixing of images that seduced ignorant viewers by the apparent naturalism of their shared looks and content. Just as the Enlighteners sought to establish their radical difference from superstitious "popish" fanatics, early Christians wished to separate themselves absolutely from the grab bag of plural gods preceding their single divinity.

James Christie, in his *Essay on That Earliest Species of Idolatry* (1814), even castigated the ecstatic "Mosaic Ceremonies" found in the Old Testament as being, in reality, a disguised worship of the personified four elements.[27] It is not accidental that the founder of one of the two original auction houses in Europe (the other being Samuel Baker of Sotheby's)[28] was interested in the nature of spectatorship and spectacle management, old and new.

Modern Free-Masons, I propose, were the descendants of the ancient "Eclectics."[29] This international network of initiates worked in secret to establish religious tolerance and to distill a common theology out of many local practices. The Baron d'Hancarville, himself a most peculiar adventurer, popularized the view of the earliest Greeks, and indeed the remnants of humanity who survived the aftermath of the biblical Flood, as animating rocks, trees, columns.[30] The trauma of this global destruction and renovation, he and others argued, was commemorated in the shadow plays of the Eleusinian mysteries, the ghostly heroes and gods decorating Greek black or red figure vases (fig. 9), the Chinese feast of the glowing lanterns, and, more generally, in what Silvestre de Sacy termed the Eastern "mystères du paganisme."[31] Perhaps earlier and more extensively than anyone else, d'Hancarville was responsible for reformulating and illustrating the principles of philhellenic syncretism for the modern era.

These "Oriental" proclivities for a system of luminous emanations, a doctrine of wandering souls or Pythagorean metempsychosis, and a firmament crowded with bright angels and dark demons, blossomed uncontrollably by the close of the eighteenth century. The desire to found a

9. [James Christie], *Red Figure Vase Depicting the Transparent "Shews at Eleusis,"* 1806.

holistic cosmopolitan order based on a common belief system all too quickly dissolved into divisive groups each with its own set of adepts and special interests. From Mesmer's channeling of the unbalanced animal spirits of *ancien régime* hysterics into supposedly therapeutic electromagnetic fields, to Madame Blavatsky's *fin-de-siècle* forays into mental telepathy, to Jung's gnostic vision of the male unconscious as stocked by a corresponding female anima and the female unconscious by a contrasting animus, the paranormal dimensions of this type of communication are what have flourished.[32]

With the approach of another millennium, apocalyptic fervor, along with reclusive electronic communes into which one must become initiated, are again proving alluring. My concern is that the impending explosion of chiliastic cults, such as the Branch Davidians and Heaven's Gate, will redraw old battle lines. While digerati celebrate the lack of restrictions, hailing the fantastic identities assumable in multiuser domains (MUDs and

MOOs) or the Zen fusions of hacker "telepathy,"[33] they also pay homage to otherworldly forces. Escapist cybergroups who remove themselves from society in order to think alike eerily resemble a militantly monotheistic early Christianity which achieved self-definition by radically denying that it shared any features with the surrounding culture. More dangerously, these fundamentalist gatherings of the faithful no longer wish to transform the world by reaching out to their opponents but are committed to the purism of remaining apart. Yet surely Katherine Anne Porter was right: there are no unmixed emotions and no exact synonyms.[34]

The issue of perceptually blending or distinguishing people, objects, or ideas gets at the specifically visual component of analogy. I want to suggest that, at a deep level, the inherent mimeticism of the method constituted its most fundamental problem, provoking intense iconoclastic or iconophilic reactions. When analogical communication was identified solely with irrational occultism—as happened during the Enlightenment—it was because vision itself had become equated, not with Cartesian clarity and rational distinctness, but with Jesuitical delusion and mystical obfuscation in general. Interestingly, key poststructuralist theorists have lately reproduced the outlines of this initially Byzantine bifurcation. For Foucault, individuals are both susceptible victims and discursively produced subjects wielding a controlling hypnotic "gaze" to seize "regimes" of power and knowledge.[35] Consider, too, the opening passage from Fredric Jameson's *Signatures of the Visible* in which he fatalistically couples vision with impotent absence of will and involuntary mesmerization by a seductive image: "The visual is essentially pornographic, which is to say that it has its end in rapt, mindless fascination; thinking about its attributes becomes an adjunct to that, if it is unwilling to betray its object, while the most austere films necessarily draw their energy from the attention to repress their own excess (rather than from the more thankless effort to discipline the viewer)."[36] Not unlike the ninth-century iconophobic emperor Constantine V,[37] Jameson negatively situates the contemporary icon within a demonic iconocracy (no longer ecclesiastically fueled, but mass-media-driven) that sustains its universalizing "diabolical" power.

In contrast to the intrinsic textuality and nonrepresentational abstractness of allegory (a major source of its appeal, I believe, to these same literary critics), analogy is a demonstrative or evidentiary practice—putting the visible into relationship with the invisible and manifesting the

10. Steve Barry, *(Our) Predilection,* 1997.

effect of that momentary unison. From the iconophilic perspective, the earthly or natural image establishes a temporary resemblance with a hidden mystery that one cannot otherwise see. All of analogy's simile-generating figures are thus incarnational. They materialize, display, and disseminate an enigma that escapes words.

Such knotty theological conundrums will be explored in chapter 3. For now I want to change registers and show through a select but diverse range of media how images analogically perform incarnation. Steve Barry's elegant installation piece *(Our) Predilection* (fig. 10), for example, illuminates the instantaneousness of this essentially visual transformation that turns dyadic into triadic relations. As the beholder looks down the barrel of a microscope, she is astonished to see her face reflected back from a mirror, not a lens. But this doubling is not exact. A pink rose—etched on the upper left side of a looking glass located at the opposite end of the table on which the microscope stands and raised perpendicular to it—is miraculously bestowed, a present from afar intimately tucked into each viewer's hair. This swift, mysterious gift works analogically since each person is different yet integrates the same attribute in a creatively individualistic way. One might say that the exchange is mutual, bringing a new person or flower to light with every perceptual transportation.

Talking about the tight clustering of objects in her installation pieces, ranging from the sinister pendulous black latex balls of *Articulated Lair* (1984) to the ethereal pharmacy *Le défi* (1991), stocked with multiform crystalline flasks and jars, Louise Bourgeois, said: "In the desolation of human relationships, I group them together, and see that they touch each other. The problem is to put every body in place, to give them a place, and especially to be sure [also] that they are together."[38] Bourgeois's sophisticated sculptural environments minimized the physical distance between disparate things of various shapes and sizes. The very different local situation of each item was both respected and altered through a parallelism that held open the possibility of eventual enfoldment. Repetition—typical of the staggered host of empty Shalimar bottles arranged on a glazed tray in her *Cell II* (fig. 11)—incarnated the insistency, insatiability, and redundancy of desire longing to move from a state of dividedness to resolution. Compulsively repeat the same container, with slight variations, and it is no longer what it once was. Similarly, Nina Levy's curtain of chain mail baubles, composed of jelly-bear torsos pivoting from toy brass meathooks, calls attention to their chromatic and expressive differences through the unnerving sameness of their form and scale (fig. 12).

Remember, too, how through the doubling and redoubling of mass-produced items such as wallpaper, with its bifurcating foliage and recurring border, or chair caning, with its airy woven interstices, the cubists transformed singular debris into tessellated still lifes. These remains of grids and scraps of arabesques—aligning order with disorder in eye-catching conjunction—constituted both the unifying bedrock and the foil for the innovative, dramatic, and equivocal patterns rising in low relief above them. Such "both/and" alchemy, transmuting generic decoration into individualized synthetic ornament, led Picasso to claim that art is "a form of magic designed as a mediator between this strange hostile world and us" (fig. 13).[39] All artifacts can become coeval when their contradictions are recomposed or reconfigured.

Creating correlatives across antitheses is also a central feature of body

11. Louise Bourgeois, *Cell II,* 1991.

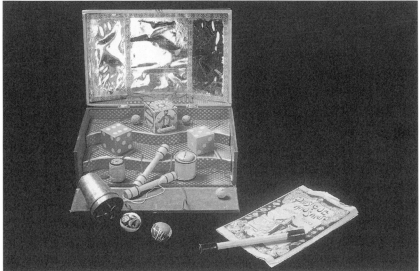

12. Nina Levy, *Curtain,* 1995.

13. N. K. Atlas, Paris, publisher, *Children's Magic Box with Instructions,* 1915–1920.

14. Raphael, *The Miraculous Draught of Fishes,*
1515.

art. Take the Renaissance case study of stunning parallelism: the arms of
Raphael's two men bending to haul up a net in his tapestry cartoon, the
Miraculous Draught of Fishes (fig. 14). Twin shapes merge into a single wa-
tery likeness in the thirdness of their combined, bluish reflection. A similar
triangulation occurs in *The Healing of the Lame Man* where the grace of
impulsive youth (St. John) and the ungainliness of wizened deformity (the
cripple) are sympathetically bound together in a complex hieroglyphic, an-
chored in the grave rectitude of the mature St. Peter (fig. 15). Analogical
procedures in the Renaissance thus held open the promise of binding human beings closer to an invisible transcendent truth.[40]

 This uncanny visual capacity to bring divided things into unison or
span the gap between the contingent and the absolute illustrates why analogy is a key feature of discernment. As perceptual judgment, it helps us

15. Raphael, *The Healing of the Lame Man,* 1515.

form ideas of elusive sensuous qualities and ephemeral emotions.[41] Not surprisingly, then, forging synesthetic links is crucial to child development as well as to the insights of scientific discovery. Inspired inferences knit perceptiveness to conceptualization by collecting the dispersed manifold into a whole. Not just the stuff of fairytales, the imaginative labor of making a coherent mermaid (by fitting the heads and tails of different species together) is symbolic of how knowledge formation actually works (fig. 16).[42] Since the task of relating human consciousness to an artifact-littered reality is unending, so is the analogical process.

The abiding conundrum of how to reach an agreement between disputants or to weigh competing claims or to discover appropriate affinities among diverse racial and ethnic groups or to tie innovation to repetition continues to haunt postmodern existence. Since the concept of analogy, in recent times, has either been simplified beyond recognition into tautology or become tainted (as I proposed earlier) through relentless identification with mystical pantheism, theosophical synchronicity,[43] and empathetic quackery of the Hollywood variety, I want to sketch key areas of contem-

16. Nina Levy, *Girlfriend,* 1997.

porary life that cry out for a fine-grained formulation of resemblance and distinction. This panoramic survey looks across today's fissured intellectual landscape, riddled with multiple yet inconclusive perspectives.[44]

Political reflection in the United States for the last fifty years, as Alan Ryan commented, has been obsessed by questions of inequality.[45] Pertinent to the theme of similarity-in-difference is the difficulty that rationalist defenders of an egalitarian theory of social justice, including John Rawls and Ronald Dworkin, are having in deciding which of the inequities swirling so visibly around us are just or unjust. The problem is that believing in the premise of social equality does not mean everyone is actually the same. The problem for law is that, currently, the concept of similarity has dissolved into the sum of correspondences and differences, commonalities and distinctions.[46]

This trend to mathematize the law, that is, to represent legal norms either according to an exaggerated Aristotelian concept of similarity as a literal economic or geometrical equality or, more radically, by positing that certain mathematical formulae are isomorphic with certain types of behavior,[47] does not begin to get at the subtleties of equal worth. A few voices are making explicit the depersonalizing poverty of this zero-sum procedure by denying that the legal hermeneutic moment consists of a symbolic logic in which two opposing, or incommensurable, entities are placed in quantitative relation. How do we go about representing a basic human dignity that deserves respect from lawmakers? William Miller has written eloquently that the qualitative emotion of shame, "lost in guilt's shadow, has been unjustly ignored as the underlying cause of most modern and postmodern psychic misery and malaise."[48]

Isaiah Berlin, Judith Shklar, and, more recently, Avishai Margalit countered the formal, calculative rationality of a social theory founded in game theory and econometrics with what might be called an analogical-existentialist perspective. In various ways, they challenge John Rawls's neo-Kantian model of a just society by asking if such an ideal is reconcilable with the existence of debasing institutions. Theirs is a humanizing vision that goes beyond the disembodied abstraction of asking what kind of a social contract rational persons would sign up for as fair terms of cooperation. By drawing attention to the noncerebral experiences of being better or worse off (for example, Berlin on the coercive totalitarianism lurking within Kant's moral imperative,[49] Shklar on the need to balance the virtues,[50] and Margalit on taking into account particular feelings of honor and humiliation so we can build a "decent society" that encompasses groups with competing and not merely incompatible types of life),[51] these authors point out, but do not resolve, the crisis of disparity mutilating the postindustrial state. Importantly, however, their pragmatic emphasis on the determining role of context in exemplary reasoning[52] highlights the connection between analogical legal methodology and humanistic, social, and scientific thinking.

This ethical tension between what Stephen Toulmin called "clean-slate" rationalism and a practical reasonableness[53] gains from being stated analogically. How can one go about establishing a connection between thinking about unequal social arrangements in terms of remote first-order principles and sensing them close-up, in terms of suffering inflicted by individual human beings on one another? Amy Gutmann makes a powerful case for the importance of reciprocity in modern deliberative democracies. Both a moral and a procedural activity, reciprocity is the way we justify mutually binding laws to one another and thus a fair way of running society.[54] In an era when moral disagreements are further fanned by scarcity of resources, limited generosity, partial understanding, and incompatible values, only the analogical procedure of discussion can help us deliberate and communicate with one another.

Turning to another major conflict dividing public opinion, when Dr. Ian Wilmut, an Edinburgh embryologist, announced that he had created a lamb from the DNA of a ewe by means of nuclear transplantation cloning, the ensuing discussions ran the gamut from legal issues (whether clones would have the same status and rights as other people), to the medieval quandary over soul-splitting, to worries about vindicating a culture of narcissism, to the specter of eugenics (the opportunity of engineering "the perfect child").[55] What was, and still is, missing from this impoverished polemic, and from that surrounding the new asexual birth technologies in general, is a sophisticated representational taxonomy recognizing the existence of *degrees* of likeness. These range from the simulacrum and facsimile, or the exact and complete replication of another thing in all its surface detail, to the subtle gradations of mimesis, best captured in the fine-grained art historical terminology separating copy from imitation, re-creation from likeness.

The imputation of an artwork's too-close resemblance to a prototype colors the long and vexed relationship between the ancients and the moderns. A flourishing eighteenth-century market in prints, especially, exposed the dilemma of our skill in creating likenesses of people and things that had first appeared in other media. The Irish painter Nathaniel Hone the Elder, for example, likened the uncontrollable proliferation of unique old master pictures through reproductive engravings to a kind of pernicious conjuring (fig. 17). The painting makes satirical reference to Joshua Reynolds's penchant for borrowing attitudes from famous continental artists and his wizardry in transforming dog-eared prints into English portraits.[56] Further, a recurring paradox of neoclassical statuary was its bondage to prior example. As Christopher Johns has shown in his study of Canova's marble statue of *Letitia Bonaparte* (1804–1807), the jealous French art establishment was quick to accuse the great Venetian sculptor of using a cast of the Capitoline Agrippina in his life-size portrait of the emperor's mother.[57]

Bioethicists, I think, could learn much from the venerable aesthetic practice of subtly varying a type. Just as the fallacy of genetic determinism

17. Nathaniel Hone the Elder, *The Conjuror,* 1775.

is to suppose that genes completely make the organism,[58] so it is a mistake to believe that identical artistic types produce identical representations. We have learned from DNA sampling techniques that even monozygotic twins are not precisely the same.[59] In the extreme case of Dolly's cell cloned by Dr. Wilmut, it is important to remember that, as it divided, it developed first into a mass of "totipotent" cells having the ability to become any kind of sheep cell, not just a mammary cell like the one that was cloned.

Similarly, the subtleties of copying also help us understand how reperforming any past or previous phenomenon brings it back into a different life. Canova's sculpture not only exhibits the complexity inherent in any binary pairing but shows how change happens, voluntarily or involuntarily, when one goes through the motions of redrawing. While he had *Madame Mère* appear in the guise of a generic Roman matron, this doubling still

18. Anonymous, *Pyramid and Sphinx at Gizeh,*
1860–1889.

left room for significant departures. Far from making a carbon copy of the totality of a distant original, he personalized the likeness of his subject, somatically distinguishing her from the parent source. Similarly, mid-nineteenth-century albumen photographs of the great pyramid and sphinx at Giza—intended for home viewing through a megalethoscope (fig. 18)—were reconceived as startlingly emotive silhouettes in early twentieth-century games of *ombres chinoises* (fig. 19). That is, just as cloned cells need to be coaxed into growing into a mass of specific tissues, like heart muscle cells or skin cells, any reproduced image passes through intermediary steps that necessarily alter its look, role, and function. In addition, the intervention of a later hand or apparatus rematerializes a prior figure that has become either formulaic or symbolic, proving its validity anew for a current situation.

19. Jean Kerhor, *L'Empéreur: Théâtre d'Ombres,*
c. 1910.

Similitude is not identity, since the prototype—whether in art or biology—undergoes continuous development from its original conception
through subsequent incarnations as a consequence of the environments or
gestures through which it passes. Consider the copy-laden *Self-Portrait* by
the eighteenth-century Irish artist James Barry (fig. 20), which is a particularly flamboyant embodiment of such kinetic knowledge, demonstrating
that to understand remarkable works one has to recreate their elements.
Thus Barry reproduced the feet of the tormented priest from the famous
Hellenistic sculptural group, the *Laocoön.* Yet these limbs were permuted
by his own subjectivity—without violating the spirit of the piece—by being depicted as more colossal than in the sculpture; similarly, the head of
the serpent was rendered more ferocious. The nexus of references crisscrossing this complex composition also involved a picture internal to the
larger picture. Alluding to a renowned rhetorical trope, the about-to-be-
flayed Pan (who is the subject of the canvas leaning against the easel) hides
his face to express the intensity of corporeal suffering, not through
wracked features but through the Belvedere twist of the torso alone.

20. James Barry, *A Self-Portrait as Timanthes,*
c. 1803.

21. William Hamilton, *Specimens of "Curious Stones" Found by Author on Mount Vesuvius,* 1776.

Among the notable things accomplished by this elaborate, partial transfer of artifacts from one sphere into another was the visible emulation of earlier masters by a recent one while, at the same time, opening up an arena for personal originality.

Barry overtly imitated the celebrated practice of the Greek painter Timanthes—recorded by Pliny—who depicted extreme pain by indirection. Although appropriating the method invented by his distinguished precursor, Barry managed to be inventive by translating old marble, pigment, and text into a new and coherent configuration. Artistic performance, like mathematical performance,[60] then, required doing the equations or repeating the gestures oneself to gain insight. This process acknowledges that not everything can be gotten at one go: the more intricate the evidence, the more restagings and approximations are necessary to assimilate it.

Turning to natural history, Peter Fabris, who was Sir William Hamilton's illustrator for the monumental two-volume *Campi Phlegraei* (1776), or scientific study of Mt. Vesuvius and Naples's "flaming fields," arranged the tufa, lava, sulfur, and pumice ejected by that volcano as if these rough specimens were intricately wrought rarities (fig. 21). A century later, a luminous magic lantern slide of American manufacture offered a haunting reprise of

22. Anonymous, *Magic Lantern Slide Depicting*
Coral Display, mid-19th century.

an assemblage of corals, madrepores, and waving fronds framed as an artful
still-life composition (fig. 22). The gray transparency of the glass evoked
a silvery and brittle underwater world whose mutability was now forever
immutable. In contrast to such arrested moments of early photography,
Fabris's brilliant, hand-colored aquatints constituted a situated science of
the visible. They chronicled the simultaneously top-down and bottom-up
emergence of layered deposits caused by firework eruptions extending
back to the dawn of time and still continuing today (fig. 23).[61] Multiple
plates coordinated the distributed activity of these sublime topographies
by creating a parallel chromatic physicality and a corresponding developmental temporality, laid out in a sequence on two-dimensional planes.

Returning again to Canova: invention was the reiteration, with a difference, of a familiar excellence. Such emulation of admirable precedents
lay at the heart of academic art education (fig. 24). The artist, relying on
canonic models and time-honored rules, selected and combined preexisting elements into more effective compositions.[62] Barry's transformation,

23. William Hamilton, *View of the Great Eruption of Mount Vesuvius on Sunday Night August the 8th 1779*, 1779.

24. Nathaniel Hone the Elder, *Horace Hone Sketching*, c. 1775.

25. H. J. F. Berg, *Man Reclining,* 1848.

within limits, of the details of venerable objects also drew on the beholder's analogizing power, his or her capacity to discern synecdochic connections between fragments from the past and the disjunctive appearances of the present. Similarly, Fabris's natural history prints converted seriality into co-presence, permitting the viewer to compare interactive portions of the real world with their ongoing pictorial embodiment.

The goal of radical originality espoused by the romantics, on the contrary, claimed for artistic innovation the right to produce entirely unknown objects and to evoke rare emotions. Hence the attraction of opium and pasha-inspired opulence for northern Europeans (fig. 25) and the lure of Byronic journeys to hot, barbaric lands (fig. 26). Postmodernism, in turn, flaunts the cold appearance of the lack of originality, especially in photographic montage and bricolage. Cindy Sherman's ironic self-portraits, dressed as Caravaggio's *Bacchus* or Raphael's *Fornarina,* blatantly restage celebrated artistic prototypes. Nonetheless, by the raw superimposition of "old masters" onto her female body, she overwhelms us with the impression that they literally "do not fit" and that gender constitutes *the* difference.[63] Borrowing a strategy basic to nineteenth-century physiognomic

26. Eugène Delacroix, *A Turk Surrenders to a Greek Horseman,* 1856.

27. Anonymous, *Cards with Physiognomy Cutouts,*
early 19th century.

games—the application of different noses or eyes to a standard template (fig. 27)—she turns the removable mask (figs. 28, 29) into a technological prosthesis behind whose engulfing artificiality lies no "true" face.

The freakish flawlessness of recent photography with digital doctoring, however, has raised greater anxieties than Cindy Sherman's or Sherrie Levine's deliberate mimicry. Worries about where reality lies are analogous to those troubling citizens concerned about the seamlessness of cloning. Artists (typically associated with the fashion industry) like David LaChapelle, Nick Knight, Inez van Lamsweerde, Jean-Baptiste Mondino, and Jean-Paul Goude pervasively and imperceptibly morph, retouch, or even totally create arresting images that do not preexist their computerization. When Mia Sorvino posed for *Allure* magazine, she thought she was appearing as Marlene Dietrich. After the shoot, LaChapelle digitally altered her features, adding the thick eyebrows and cruel lips of Joan Crawford and superimposing an axe-wielding child model playing Cristina Crawford next to her.[64] Clearly, the sanctity of the negative has vanished.

28. H. F. Müller, *Everyone Wears Masks* (face covered), 1790–1820.

29. H. F. Müller, *Everyone Wears Masks* (face uncovered), 1790–1820.

After the initial furor over Dolly's genetic "xeroxing" subsided, scientists, too, rushed to say that "a duplicate body does not mean a duplicate person. The clone's brain would be far different from that of the donor, as it must start from scratch and build its own world of experiences."[65] This Lockean thesis about learning from the senses gains in force when put in terms of visual analogy. Something cannot be an image except in relation to an original. Plato, in the *Sophist*, declared that "to be an image" is to have a unique look, to possess a defining mark that both connects and disconnects this repetition to a family of cases.[66] While Dolly's body is an undisguised re-creation—like Sherman's notorious attachments worn as if they were masks—her brain is not a redundancy but an approximate image, that is, an imitation. Something significant is left over and cannot be totally incorporated back into the system that generated her. This is patently not the case with digital enhancement, where efficient manipulation ensures that there is no tell-tale remainder in the resulting simulation. Because of the role played by the external environment in learning, Dolly, on the contrary, is simultaneously like and unlike her chronologically prior, but not ontologically superior, "maternal" source.

The dilemma of identical appearances confronts us wherever we look. International disagreements about maintaining "genetic purity" or creating animal hybrids are surfacing among managers of zoos and wildlife parks. The previous interbreeding of the eastern and southern black rhinoceros or the Bengal and Indochinese tiger or the Bornean and Sumatran orangutan is forcing biologists to reconsider the fundamental question of how they categorize living things and their transformations. Are formal changes absolute or graduated? Do you artificially lump subspecies and species together, thus "contaminating" them, or do you split them into an endless series based on barely perceptible differences?[67] These disputes highlight both the absence of a method for judging how distinct a subspecies must be to be considered separate and the danger of abstracting any living being from its environmental context.

Contemporary researchers inventing hybrids might find D'Arcy Thompson's "principle of similitude," articulated in his 1917 book *On Growth and Form*, illuminating. Emphasizing the functional aspect of form rather than heredity, he argued that an organism should be regarded as a material and mechanical configuration. Morphology, therefore, is not only a study of stable material things, but of their mutable and comparative aspects. "Dynamic similarity" maps the forces in action across an entire system such that some vary as one power and some as another. Their relational values fluctuate with shifts in scale.[68] He remarked how slower and calmer motions in animals can be correlated with larger size. Proportionality, the establishment of a geometrical ratio between speed and magnitude, constitutes the cornerstone of his physicomathematical theory of shape.

Thompson's vision of the universe was deeply, and at the time unfashionably, analogical: embracing an infinity of great and small, near and far, many and few items, all demanding to be placed in commerce with one another. The effect of dimension (or, one might add, the issue of experimentally induced border-crossings versus maintaining genetically pristine stock) depends not on the species itself but on its changing relation to the shifting milieu.

Similarly, the distinguished twentieth-century Aristotelian René Thom concluded his study on "the physics of the senses" by asserting that modern science is wrong in renouncing the importance of ontology in the production of biological meaning and reducing all criteria of truth to limited, local solutions.[69] As Thompson urged, only by comparing and contrasting the forms assumed by matter under all guises and conditions (including forms that are only theoretically or mathematically imaginable) is it possible to arrive at correspondences in function between organs or parts of different structures. Only then may we witness how every natural phenomenon is really a composite, the summation of countless subordinate actions.[70]

Modern biology, contrary to the situation in Thompson's day, is armed with a computer able to sort out the affinities of different creatures based on a statistical comparison of their objective measurements. This electronic capacity to correlate vast quantities of data has led to the discovery of exciting homologies. Unlike analogy (in biology, a correspondence in function between organs or different parts of different organisms), homology is the discovery of a fundamental similarity in structure—regardless of function—due to descent from a common ancestor. In cladistics, exhibiting homology has led to the surprising revelation of the unnaturalness of certain old categories such as that of reptiles—which puts lizards and crocodiles in proximity. But it has also revealed the naturalness of placing crocodiles closer to birds than to their erstwhile companions. Cows and worms, in this homologous system, share unexpected features indicating that the great forms of life that supposedly burst into existence during the Cambrian explosion five hundred and fifty million years ago actually were born long before then.

The crucial problem of determining the proper relationship between underlying laws and explicit results also fuels the acrimonious charges hurled by "Darwinian fundamentalists" against "nonadaptive pluralists."[71] Stephen Jay Gould has taken Daniel Dennett, in particular, to task for denying any importance to chance and contingency in the history of life. A proponent of punctuated equilibrium, Gould claims that the ultra-Darwinian insistence on natural selection as the sole valid mechanism for evolution does not do justice to the fact that organisms are complex and highly integrated. This coherence suggests, to him, that they must throw off "spandrels" or structural byproducts that may become useful at a later point in evolutionary development.[72]

His evocative analogy derives from architecture and refers to the supplemental triangular space remaining between the exterior curve of an arch and the enclosing right angle, as seen most famously in Michelangelo's Sistine Chapel ceiling. Helena Cronin refers to "likeness in diversity," the power of many small changes to pull organisms into line and shape them over vast stretches of time by a selective force that is both opportunistic and conservative.[73] To borrow an analogy from hypermedia, evolution—like human cognition—has a nonlinear structure permitting the organism to navigate along random and multiple pathways and to choose options by making associative links.

Reconciling and integrating the random, nonadaptive aspects of evolutionary change with its determinate, universal side must also infuse thinking about consciousness and how the brain works.[74] Here, disturbingly, the physiognomic fallacy has returned. Localizing mental operations into discrete organs has mesmerized evolutionary psychology. Steven Pinker has expanded his "toolbox" model of the mind into the argument that natural selection shaped a general intelligence in humans, and that specific mental skills also evolved rather than resulting from the application of intelligence.[75] He thus attempts to synthesize the computational view of the mind as software that turns information into manipulable symbols with the view that mental abilities, akin to organisms, arose through natural selection.

The concept of modularity—like Lavater's rigid identification of psychic states with specific facial features (fig. 30)[76] or Gall's and Spurzheim's cranial grids—is once again being used to minutely anatomize behavior. There is a long and dubious history of trying to coordinate absolutely internal or mentalized phenomena with externalized anatomy.[77] Now, noninvasive imaging devices have gone far beyond measuring the phrenological terrain of the skull. Neural geography has sunk deep within the cortex, arousing hopes of correlating isolated perceptual and cognitive functions with equally separate regions of the brain. The danger looms that adaptive significance will be postulated for individual memes or units without consideration of context—in line with a hard-wired Darwinian approach. Yet variation needs to be "blind" in order to be productive, not just reproductive. The imagination itself is analogous to biological evolution in that it requires the unpredictable generation of a rich diversity of alternatives and conjectures.

The pressing need for constructing appropriate affinities (evident, as I outlined, in legal studies, biotechnology, population genetics, and evolutionary theory) also lies at the heart of communication. In light of the widespread public wariness about the humanities, Gerald Graff remarked that the competitive relation between academic and nonacademic forms of popular culture has made it difficult to see their points of commonality. The gulf, however, stretches not between teaching Madonna or Henry James. The real opposition yawns between media culture and the culture of academic argumentation.[78] This unequal competition for the attention of our students is exacerbated by the increasing impossibility of organizing modular departments and "interdisciplinary" curricula around a consensus on what should be taught and why. As fine as it is, Graff's suggestion to "teach the conflicts"[79] is not enough. Without a coordinating method for arriving at principled agreement, isolated monologues, disconnected disciplines, and unresolved conflicts will continue to make universities both incoherent to ourselves and unintelligible to our disaffected constituency.

Take a case from the "orientalist" wars. The incompatibilities thwarting intercultural dialogue can be exemplified, at one level, as the Asian struggle to pursue a cosmopolitan dream of integration with the West while maintaining national, and even racial, independence from such a self-alienating synthesis. The problem is not new. Presenting Japan to a European audience in the late nineteenth century, for example, became an

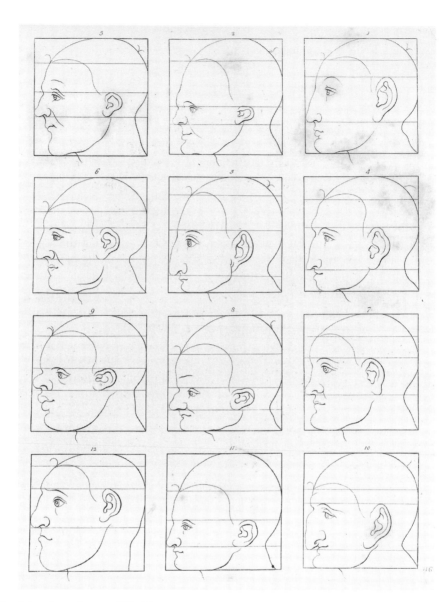

30. Johann Caspar Lavater, *Gridded Faces Revealing Disproportions,* 1791.

act of cultural betrayal and dispossession since, as Shigemi Inaga has argued, Japanese artists abroad could only make their mark by playing up their essential "Japaneity," i.e., by conforming to someone else's representation of themselves.[80] The quandary, then as well as now, he claims, is that this denies their desire to be seen as international when traveling far from home. Inaga concludes that the assumption of a pose for another has the traumatic consequence of putting the Japanese in a role not of variable individuals, but of representatives of a static tradition.

Does such fatalism and disjointedness determine how the scenario must be played out? As it stands, it does, and not only for this specific instance but for cross-cultural contacts of all sorts. "Minority histories," as Dipesh Chakrabarty has written, tend to be oppositional chiefly in the early stage of their careers. As soon as they become incorporated into mainstream accounts, they end up being instances of "good history." Yet this still leaves open the case of "subaltern pasts," i.e., all those past oral traditions that can never completely enter the contemporary historian's space, not because of any wish to marginalize them, but because they represent incongruent moments.[81] By definition, the ethnographic archive is always out of synchronization with the Western researcher exploring it. But couldn't this be said of any historical inquiry?

Without a sophisticated theory of analogy, there is only the negative dialectics of difference, ending in the unbreachable impasse of pretended assimilation or the self-enclosed insistence on absolute identity with no possibility for meaningful communication. Analogizing has the virtue of making distant peoples, other periods, and even diverse contemporary contexts part of our world. Only by making the past or the remote or the foreign proximate can we hope to make it intelligible to us. I want to counter Inaga's dichotomous logic, then, by considering how Pacific Rim computer users have evolved a different set of emoticons from their Atlantic cousins. These are the strange combinations of punctuation, accent marks, and letters used in electronic mail to indicate happiness, sadness, and other feelings. Japanese double-byte (unlike our single-byte) smileys are intricate in design, oblique in their expression, and right side up instead of sideways.[82]

Accustomed to looking at compound pictograms, the Japanese have developed an elaborate hieroglyphics of face marks that allusively conjoin words to complex, and even vague, emotions such as: breaking out in a cold sweat (^^), excuse me (^O^;>), or a wide "banzai" cheer \(^O^)/. This rich graphic range greatly exceeds the schematism of Bill Gates's Internet combinatory. Far from positing an East-West isomorphism, the Noh mask emoticons simultaneously allude to Japan's court theater while retaining a structural resemblance to the Euro-American version to facilitate global communication. Slipping an individualized physiognomy over a generic type is a practice central to Western caricature. Remember Daumier's habit of superimposing the bulbous and jowly Louis-Philippe onto a cheeky pear, leading to the mutual transformation of king and fruit.

Douglas Cardinal, architect of the new National Museum of the American Indian on the Mall in Washington, D.C., offers yet another impasse-dissolving alternative to the discourse of cultural binaries by viewing space as a dynamic continuum inflected by sculpted objects. A descendant of the Blackfoot and Métis, Cardinal develops organic analogies to the sinuous, curvilinear spirals of seashells and mounded sand dunes in his futurist designs so that they resonate with the earth. As the NMAI project coalesces, the architect's work tables are ringed by photographs of cryptic petroglyphs from the Southwest, carved sandstone canyons, the indigenous abstraction of Anasazi cliff dwellings, and rugged Alpine escarpments.[83] These "natural masterpieces"[84] serve as potent reminders of how to conjoin ancient landscape with modern city, looming rock outcrop with concrete monument. Like the late work of Le Corbusier, notably the chapel of Notre-Dame du Haut at Ronchamp (1950–1955), Cardinal's curvilinear forms function "acoustically"[85] as a visual echo of the surrounding vista. He shows how matter and energy interconnect, how the spiritual energy emanating from the unbuilt environment can animate and irradiate an otherwise inert habitat.

Finally, making connections and creating coherence are nowhere more at stake than in the on-line treasure hunt that has users desperately searching for meaning through the "data smog."[86] Trawling through the confusing and largely unstandardized array now available on screen has the frustrated seeker clamoring for what can only be called an analogical tool. An ideal browser would provide access to global sources and aid in the responsible incorporation of structured with unstructured information. The World Wide Web continues to revolutionize the ways in which anonymous people and downloaded files get cobbled together. It constitutes a new cosmic force field in which all phenomena become artificial variables in a vast cyberwave of continuously emitting energy. Researchers disembodiedly share far-flung apparatus, libraries and museums electronically display their delocalized collections, opening them to interactive use, colleges provide access to courses taught at a distance, and just about everyone pools their deracinated findings without assigning origin or credit. Yet our higher educational system has yet to integrate the imagistic universe of multimedia with printed books. Nor has it made it a top priority to investigate the complications arising when historically validated organizational schemes mutate or are eliminated.[87] Along with the joys, the frustrations of navigating the Internet point out that to make useful information available we need an equally big, rich, and complex method for creating, judging, and discriminating among tightly integrated hybrid linkages.

The global village is growing increasingly factionalized. Witness the explosion of biometrics or recognition technology.[88] Face identification, hand geometry, and iris scanning indicate that all is not well in cyberland. These batches of digital devices that recognize people through various physical characteristics—faces, hands, fingers, eyes, voices—are an anxious response to the computer's voracious and amoral capacity to gather all kinds of data, including the most personal. Not only does this automated power to accumulate images of bits and pieces of our bodies raise legitimate privacy concerns, but it leaves unanswered the question of just who is going synthesize this endless miscellany of emanations. Unlike the transmission of light or sound waves in a controlled ambient, the computer and its three-dimensional extensions like the ImmersaDesk and CAVE—as the latest versions of the universe in a box (fig. 31)—have erased the hope that this rear-projected imagery will be equally received by all (fig. 32).

How, then, do we craft a coordinated mosaic from this heterogeneous broadcast of splintering fragments? What search engine will help us perceive reliable resemblances? Smart equipment and commercial software are machines accessing and filtering data, not the contents of learning or the stuff of cultures. Software agents, in automatically tailoring information to highly specific individual interests, paradoxically valorize known material rather than encouraging open-ended meandering into unknown territory. The rise of a distributed approach to knowledge—spurred by computer operating systems that create databases registering users' likes or dislikes and even go on to "breed" algorithms whose survival is independent of human selection[89]—still requires a guiding intelligence to avoid lapsing

31. Athanasius Kircher, *Room-Sized Camera Obscura,* 1671.

32. *Virtual Reality ImmersaDesk,* 1997.

into solipsism. The mechanistic expansion of subjectivity invokes the twin specter of fragmentation and replication of interests.

The emergent panglobal idiom of multimedia conjures up memories of creative complementarity articulated in the late seventeenth-and early eighteenth-century doctrine of *ut pictura poesis*. This comparatist initiative enabled painting and poetry to coexist in a mutually supportive role by virtue of their expressive and technical correspondences.[90] Drawing and writing were conceived as equivalent components of one and the same ideogrammatic process. But, during the high Enlightenment, Lessing's adamant rejection of formal interart parallels in the *Laocoön* (1766) exerted powerful pressures to define picture-making as an art independent of architecture, sculpture, and literature. This paradigm-shifting book also established a hierarchy that set temporal genres like drama and poetry above spatialized media. Consequently, Lessing overturned a line of argument—stretching from Roger de Piles to Locke, Addison, and especially Berkeley—extolling the communicative potential of painting's iconic signs and predicting the advent of a universal "mother tongue" of synergistic appearances.

Today, irradiated pixels have once again transformed music, image, and text into a consolidated pattern. But morphing is not a harmonious interaction, nor is sensory distraction the same as a complexly synthesized vision. Electronic commerce—enabling new kinds of interactivity among networked companies and their dispersed suppliers and customers[91]—requires more than a novel set of managerial skills or the eradication of an old corporate hierarchy solidly structured around function-defined departments. It demands a hybrid knowledge composed of interwoven disciplinary content, a sophisticated awareness of the wide spectrum of existing and possible relationships among parts and wholes, and the ability to discriminate among competing choices. At the close of the twentieth century, it should give us pause that we still lack a flexible method for orchestrating the jumble of discrete emissions and darting blips that swim across countless monitors. They remain a hermetic system of graphic symbols for which we have lost the analogical key.

2

Figures of Reconciliation

> But, if you kept them separate, in many ways you saw them more truly. . . .
> One could let all these facts lie alongside each other like laminations, not
> like growing cells. This laminated knowledge produced a powerful sense
> of freedom, truthfulness and even selflessness, since the earlier and sexual
> linking by analogy was undoubtedly selfish.
> *A. S. Byatt*, The Virgin in the Garden

Biologically and emotionally, human beings are shaped for relating to their
shifting surroundings. The world's theogonies are sensuous geographies
reminding us that the body—conceived magically, cabbalistically, or
alchemically—was once buffeted by a sea of terrestrial and celestial influences (fig. 33).[1] Even in today's hermetically sealed, skyscrapered environment, the involuntary stirrings of our five senses testify to the ancient
give and take between a corporealized mind and an animate universe. Analogy is about this fundamentally participatory mode of perception.

We become aware of thinking only in those kinesthetic moments when
we actively bind the sights, savors, sounds, tastes, and textures swirling
around us to our inmost, feeling flesh. In Jusepe de Ribera's visualization
of touch, a blind man palpates the eye sockets, nose, mouth, and back of
the head of a marble bust, inferring features in the process of internalizing
shapes and surfaces through his fingers (fig. 34). In a witty *paragone*, or
comparison of the art of sculpture with that of painting, Ribera contrasts
halting knowledge, derived from the handling of a three-dimensional object over time, with the immediate intuition of seeing a coherent form. An
anamorphic portrait, lying at an angle and sharply foreshortened on a
trompe-l'oeil table top, springs from flatness into saliency in a clever optical
illusion, depending on the movement of the viewer. The Spanish artist
illuminates how this simultaneously retinal and conceptual fusion can only
be provisional. The yoking relationship has to be personally reperformed
by each beholder.

In this chapter, I want to delineate three aspects of an embodying analogy that expose its shifting historical fate within literary, artistic, and
philosophic disciplines. The first section develops the distinction between
analogy and allegory as opposed methods for relating part to whole, visible
to invisible, known to unknown, individual to culture. I suggest that, especially in the romantic use of allegory as *disanalogy*, the refusal to discriminate among competing characteristics glorified the failure even to attempt

33. Anonymous, *The Philosophical Work*, from
Occulta Philosophia, 1613.

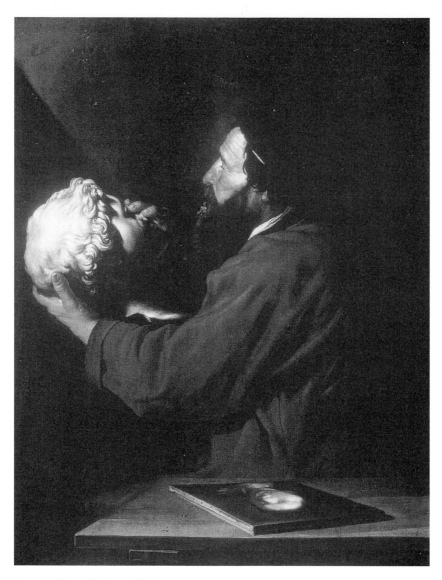

34. Jusepe de Ribera, *The Sense of Touch,*
c. 1615–1616.

such a struggle. Analogy, as the creative and tentative weaving together of individuated phenomena, was thus supplanted by the elevation of atomistic difference: the obsession with unbridgeable imparity and the hieratic insistence on insurmountable distance between the material and spiritual realms. Postmodernism has inherited romanticism's excessive skepticism, even its alternating bouts of schizophrenia and paranoia, a skepticism that finds the subject either incapable of comparing heterogeneous experiences or filtering all events through an irrational logic that renders them mystically equivalent.[2] The second section examines the different "look" or style these opposed techniques contributed to the representation of the visual world: analogy's bonding figures of reconciliation became dismembered into allegory's laminated grotesques. The third section relocates the aesthetic ramifications of analogy within a specifically philosophical tradition, noting the important and underanalyzed differences between a predicative and a participatory theory of union. Hierarchy, or the concept of the procession of multitudinous beings from a single God and their reversion to his all-embracing Oneness, formed a cosmic dialectic between transcendence and belonging.

Since analogy demands that we take seriously the problem of correlation, it is central both to ancient religions and to a modern anthropology of the senses.[3] I want to recuperate the lost link between visual images and concepts, the intuitive ways in which we think simply by visualizing. The evolution of embodied thought—from chimpanzee to man—consists in the power to create similes. The capacity to generalize to new objects from those already encountered is based on perceiving common traits and matching them according to a shared category.[4] Information theory is particularly interested in the role played by inferencing in problem solving and how analogy not only compares mental representations but inductively regroups them into new coordinations.[5]

While much has been written about metaphor or metonymy, the attention paid to organic analogy as an associative *method* has been scant and sporadic since the late eighteenth century. As we shall see, what writings exist are largely to be found in the history of philosophy and cosmogony. Unifying analogy was periodically superseded by fragmenting allegory— a fate that already overtook it in late antiquity. But the seventeenth century changed everything, compulsively accentuating difference at the expense of alliances. There is a trajectory arcing from Hobbes's and Descartes's failed dream of boundless self-sufficiency and mental autonomy to the romantic's despair at finding a real likeness in unlike things.

One of the central goals of German post-Enlightenment and Counter-enlightenment[6] philosophy was to find some inner unity that might bridge Kant's "Platonic" division of the unknowable thing-in-itself from the practical moral realm.[7] The noble failure of this generation of thinkers of the mid-1780s and 1790s—chiefly Jacobi, Hamann, Herder, Schleiermacher, Fichte, and Friedrich Schlegel—to avoid the solipsistic relativism brought on by Hume's devastating attack on causality only resulted in a heightened dichotomy. This acute awareness that there seemed to be no necessary and universal connection between accidentally repeated sense impressions left the mind confronting an abyss. Either it was doomed to a rational skepticism verging on nihilism or it had to commit to an irrational leap of faith. That is, either reality was out there and we knew it because, in fact, our imagination had created it, or all of creation was an enigmatic hieroglyphic, an allegory containing the secret symbolic message of God to which we have no privileged access.

Not surprisingly, the romantics pondered the ambiguities arising in the attempt to divine the unknown from the known, the inner essence from the outer appearance. Schleiermacher, in particular, reflected on methods of prognostication. He pushed the ancient interpretive conundrum of how, with certainty, to scan the planets for revelations, or foretell fate from a tangle of entrails, or decipher the cracks on a tortoise shell, back to the intractable bedrock of the concealed subject. As Kierkegaard was later to do, Schleiermacher claimed that every human being remained an enigma. We can only intuit, not rationally comprehend, the riddle of the inmost self. One's intrinsic personhood is an inscrutable foreign country, inaccessible to the outsider except by inference.[8]

In his radical retreat from representation, articulated in the 1799 lectures *Über die Religion*, Schleiermacher inspired a decisive shift among the German romantics from aesthetics to religion.[9] This direct, "spiritual sense" of infinity pushed synthesizing analogical awareness toward anti-ocular Gnostic allegory. Whatever apprehension of the universe this "pure" intuition might provide, it offered no representation of it. Ironically, both in the ancient and modern versions of this prophesying epistemology, the divine no longer mediated human experience, since man had become the solitary manufacturing agent of solely fictional worlds.

Friedrich Schlegel, in 1796, joined his Neoplatonist compatriot Novalis in radically dichotomizing the theory of representation. His political assessment of the possibilities for a harmonious republicanism in a post-revolutionary democracy also applied to romantic poetics. The absolutely general will, he declared, "does not occur in the realm of experience, and exists only in the world of pure thought. The individual and the universal are therefore separated from each other by an infinite gulf. . . . There is no solution here other than, by means of a fiction, to regard an empirical will as the surrogate of the a priori absolute general will."[10] As Wilhelm von Humboldt put it in his 1821 address on "The Task of the Historian," this fictionalizing of any overarching principle, or assertion of a total hermeneutic gap between types of being, means that no understanding can span the varieties of existence.[11]

Since I am claiming that an allegorization of interpretation has steadily been overwhelming its analogical counterpart since Descartes's derivation of knowledge from the clear and distinct establishment of contrasts between things, to reach a crisis with the romantics' nominalist construction of the universe, we need to look at both terms more carefully. Allegory belongs to a whole class of rhetorical devices sharing two traits. These work by an exploitation of difference, rather than by establishing an underlying likeness, and they deliberately pursue "darkness" or obfuscation rather than clarity. This *diversiloquium* is most closely aligned with the opaque figures of irony, enigma, and riddle, that is, with an exaggerated and puzzling way of saying one thing and meaning another.[12] It might help, then, to think of allegory as a type of heightened disanalogy[13] which, instead of focusing on characteristics that two or more items share, insist upon what they do not share.

Unlike sudden and "flashy" analogy, as Thomas Blackwell remarked in his *Letters Concerning Mythology* (1748), allegory is cool, abstracted, without the passion and warmth of simile's impulse to connect.[14] While it has been customary to point out the supposed hatred Wordsworth or Blake felt for allegory as opposed to symbol, Thomas Vogler and Michael Murrin have commented how the romantic symbol, in fact, resembles an elevated definition of allegory.[15] The recent, and long overdue, reevaluation of the relationship between romanticism and the "metaphysicals" of the seventeenth century has linked Ann Radcliffe's Gothicism to Milton's Satan and Hell and demonstrated Coleridge's affinities with John Donne.[16]

The romantics, in their hyperbolic Neoplatonism, pushed the spiritualization of the symbol, its *allos* or "otherness," to the point where material signs and immaterial significance occupied the antipodes. When every single thing dotting the universe was considered so distinctively individual as to be its own symbol, there was no opportunity to traverse these unconditional differences through resembling degrees. Instead, any movement to establish correspondences required an irrational leap of faith.

Philipp Otto Runge's (1777–1810) large, incomplete *Morning* presents just such a symbolical mosaicized composition, grounded in mirror symmetry and the stark repetition of self-same fragments (fig. 35). This divisionist absence of in-betweenness is exhibited in the brusque juxtaposition of the two infant genii flanking the central figure of Aurora. Each being—whether angelic putto or luminous goddess—inhabits his or her patch of blue, separated by an unpainted and disconnected square of canvas. In the smaller, completed version (dating from 1807) faint, leaflike emanations tenuously climb upward from the radiant landscape to vanish within the azure empyrean arching above them. To see these phantom tendrils at all, the viewer has to stand almost flush with the edge of the picture and peer into the translucent sky.

The great pictures in the Hamburger Kunsthalle offer a lesson in romantic allegorism as the reification of dissimilarity. The awkwardness of the asymmetrically arranged *Hülsenbeck Children*, for example, derives from the conspicuous lack of a middle term (fig. 36). The grouping is blatantly arithmetical: $1 + 2 = 3$. These fleshed integers are arbitrarily tied together by a long run of identical, globe-topped fence posts and by the redoubled red and yellow shoes worn by the two older boys. Similarly, in the life-size *Portrait of His Parents*, accompanied by Runge's two sons Sigismund and Ernst standing in the foreground, the absolute incongruity between youth and age is expressed not only by disproportions in appearance but by shocking discrepancies in scale (fig. 37).

After such antinomian romantic works, it is a shock to encounter Jan Steen's inventive variations on the seventeenth-century theme of the *Merry Company*. These sophisticated genre paintings depicted roistering families democratically incorporating everyone from howling babies to bibulous grandparents. Runge's distinguishing dualism systematically inverted the baroque rules for assimilative ordering, still obeyed by Steen. The results,

35. Philipp Otto Runge, *Morning (Large)*,
1808–1809.

36. Philipp Otto Runge, *Hülsenbeck Children,*
1806.

in Runge, were lonely scenes in which the distance between generations
was so accentuated as to be untraversable.

Contrast, too, the rituals of English polite society in which proper relational etiquette became incarnated as an economy of finely adjusted proportions. The elevated position of the charming scion of an aristocratic
household was subtly correlated to a world of diverse adults in Sir Joshua
Reynolds's brilliant late conversation piece, *George Grenville, Marquis of
Buckingham and His Family.* The painter artificially raised the small heir
(Richard Granville, eldest son of the marquis's first marriage) on the human pedestal of an adolescent black servant in a feudal declaration of

37. Philipp Otto Runge, *Portrait of His Parents,*
1806.

primogeniture. While playfully towering above his adoring seated step-mother, the boy subtly approached by degrees, but did not exceed, the height of his proud father (fig. 38). The "family values"[17] of human attachments were evoked in the eighteenth century to ensure cohesion in a society growing more horizontal. No such adjudication obtained in Runge's steeply vertical representation, where bent, bitter, and grim elders loomed over tiny, unprotected, and innocent tots.

Caspar David Friedrich (1774–1840) amplified the disjunctures evident in Runge's figural work by exposing the noetic geometry underpinning all material forms. Georg F. Kersting's portrait of the pensive artist standing in a barren cell-like studio aptly drew attention to the cruciform window panes (repeated in the cross bars of the easel) and the parallelism of slender table or chair legs (echoed in lengthening stripes of shadow that would never meet) (fig. 39). It was Friedrich's haunting landscapes, however, consisting of solitary boats, anchors, trees, or cairns, that most conspicuously opposed objects in mirror symmetry and used them as borders for intensifying vacancy. The monumental *Seashore by Moonlight* captured two silhouetted sails, forever held motionless as though pulled taut by an invisible string, and eternally kept apart by a blank stretch of phosphorescent water (fig. 40).

But it was Friedrich's coldly crystalline *Shipwreck* that best instantiated the disanalogical "laminated" style of which Byatt wrote in the epigraph quoted at the head of this chapter (fig. 41). The Dresden painter's bleak scene, dominated by a fractured sheet of ice, mimicked upheaved geological strata that "lie alongside each other" without ever merging. These mountainous horizontal layers, like the tight clustering of vertical tree trunks in *Early Snow* (1828), or the compass-drawn solar rays forming the background of *The Burning of Neubrandenburg* (c. 1834), belong to an asexual geometry diagramming the acute loneliness of unblendable distinctions.

With this allegorization of existence the conviction of a vast "ontological difference,"[18] to use Heidegger's phrase, became so tenacious that it was impossible to conceive a viable link between a string of discrete predicates and their remote originating noun. The ever-widening chasm between phenomena and noumena, nonbeing and Being, diversity and identity, turned a rhetorical device into the key metaphysical problem of Western philosophy: the nature of the connection between a single cause

38. Joshua Reynolds, *George Grenville, Marquis of Buckingham and His Family,* c. 1780.

39. Georg F. Kersting, *Portrait of Caspar David Friedrich in His Studio,* c. 1812.

40. Caspar David Friedrich, *Seashore by Moonlight,* 1835–1836.

and plural effects. But it also marked a larger cultural shift. The allegorical turn is closely allied to the spread of cynicism,[19] the ironization of social conventions from top to bottom that intensified during and after the Enlightenment.

Just who was this allegorist? The eighteenth-century *libertin galant*, Elena Russo writes, was an essentialist, a Hobbesian free thinker, an antisocial individualist.[20] His or her (as famously in the case of the Marquis de Sade's Madame de Merteuil) neo-Stoic aspiration to exalted freedom and heightened intellectualism sounds—to my mind—a lot like the Renaissance mannered courtier and the Baudelairean detached, skeptical observer. By dint of veneering or armoring the self, these aristocrats of the spirit affirmed their superiority over others through the regulation of pose, suppression of spontaneity, and dispassionate enactment of constructed

41. Caspar David Friedrich, *Shipwreck (Polar Sea)*, 1823–1824.

roles through sheer force of will (fig. 42). The libertine's advocacy of secrecy, his autarkic desire to consort only with select initiates, represented a dissonant reaction to, and undermining of, the relational virtues of *honnêteté*.

I am suggesting that the analogist belonged to the community of *honnêtes gens* for whom social ideals were seen as reciprocal. This group found its unity in emulative norms and models sanctioned by the rules of mimesis. In this reverberating salon milieu—captured in Jean Restout's (1692–1768) unusual *Last Supper* (fig. 43) as conversation piece—the unique individual could still hope to interact and ally himself with those who were not exactly his equals. In this sociable situation, with its network of subtle bonds among a meritocracy of intimates, Christ was distinguished by his bright aura, his antithetical position across from the swarthy Judas who, significantly, was seated on the same side of the table. More significantly,

42. Titian, *Portrait of a Commander-in-Chief (Ferrante-Gonzaga?)*, c. 1552.

43. Jean Restout, *The Last Supper,* 1744.

44. Salomon de Caus, *Automaton—Cyclops
Playing Pan Pipes,* 1615.

however, Restout emphasized Jesus's companionable humanity by singling him out from, while simultaneously embedding him within, the motley band of faithful disciples in the middle ground who variously struggled to resemble him.

Such consonances temporarily transcend the war tearing apart competing subjects solely motivated by a dominating *amour-propre.* By contrast, the allegorist's contrived behavior fostered a cynical split between private consciousness and public performance, an unbridgeable rift between inner reality and outer appearance. These opposing world views also borrowed their metaphors from different domains. Artifice and calculation, cold laboratory and icy machine (fig. 44), were marshaled in the attack against organicism and procreation, blossoming garden and sheltering home (fig. 45).

If the allegorist—whether in his mannerist, libertine, or Byronic dandy incarnation (see fig. 25)—revived archaic, even feudal oppositional values of hierarchy, deference, and pedigree, the analogist belonged to the polite society of sociability that flourished and vanished with the *ancien régime.* Analogy's transformative strategy placed a premium not on absolute difference but on nuanced degrees of distinction. The upholding of

45. William Hogarth, *The Mackinen Children,*
1747.

personal identity always necessitated discovering the resemblance in two opposing views so that they might be triangulated. Unfixing polarities required a structural system of kinships—visible in the popular "conversation pieces" of the eighteenth century. Jean-François de Troy, William Hogarth, or Joshua Reynolds (see fig. 38) honored the temperamental independence of their upper- or wealthy middle-class sitters while inserting them within a tapestry of affiliations. Like analogy's liminal position in an argument, as the third term reconciling two extremes, the acrobatics of choreographed speech offered a visual way of displaying worth within a social setting founded on friendship, real proximity, and the swift juggling of divergent ideas.

Since analogy and allegory are both about dichotomous structures and involve a binary logic, they are not, and were not, easy to keep apart. At a deep level, they are the obverse and the reverse of the same coin, upholding and destroying conjunctions. In her fine analysis of Spenser's use of tropes in the *Faerie Queene*, Isabel MacCaffrey differentiated between analytical and synthetic allegory.[21] She argued that the former procedure arose when the poet entered into an extended explication of the obscure and equivocal things confronting our fallen understanding. Humanity's postlapsarian condition insured that we could no longer see meaning directly but required the syllogistic unfolding of complex concepts. The power of the imagination, the *ingenium*, to make sense of a complicated situation consisted, therefore, in "unmetaphorizing" the illusionistic duplicity accompanying our sinful state.

Analytical allegory's dissection of a corrupt from a pristine knowledge is akin, it seems to me, to the allegorized chemical symbol of German *Naturphilosophie*. The invisible revealed itself only negatively as a phosphorescent trace deposited on the visible murkiness of matter. This "practice of learned ignorance," promulgated by Nicholas of Cusa in the early fifteenth century, unleashed a fascination for nonapprehension and the truth of nothing.[22] Catherine Wagner's nine silver gelatin prints of *Sequential Molecules* capture the singular glow of this fragile and representation-eluding realm poised on the brink of evanescence (fig. 46). Synthetic allegory's attempt to relate human production to a transcendent reality, on the other hand, can be likened to analogy's transactional dialectics.

Velásquez's *Spinners* created just such a combinatorial bridge erected on similes (fig. 47). As Leonard Barkan demonstrated in his study of Ovid's

46. Catherine Wagner, *Sequential Molecules,*
1995.

47. Diego Velásquez da Silva, *The Spinners, or the Fable of Arachne,* 1657.

Metamorphoses, the pagan universe was structured according to a system of transformations permitting individuals to shuttle between divine, human, and animal incarnations. These sudden mutations provided ways to transfer personal qualities onto the impersonal physical world and vice versa.[23] Velásquez's painted fable specifically plays with this anthologizing or collecting theme of a multilayered and interconnected cosmos. The monumental picture alludes to the fierce competition between two legendary weavers: the proud mortal, Arachne, and the guileful immortal, Minerva. This tragic contest is incorporated into an apparently descriptive genre scene. The foreground is dominated by five skilled and muscular artisans typical of those employed at the Royal Tapestry Factory of Santa Isabel in Madrid. Rather more mysteriously, three women—excerpted as if caught in a faraway mirror—occupy the minuscule elevated room in the background. One gestures toward a glowing tapestry of *The Rape of Europa,* after

Titian, covering the entire rear wall. As in *Las Meninas* (1656), where Velásquez wedded his self-portrait to a scene of production in the midst of court,[24] the *Spinners* synthesizes a fragment from the supernatural realm with a natural scenario: indeed, one can be said to analogically reflect the other.

As in a woven fabric, the warp of divinity and the woof of humanity are not so much fused as braided into one another. The three central women in the foreground can be plaited into the picture both as the Fates who card, spin, and cut the thread of life and as real-life embodiments of virtuosity. Two of them further evoke the combatants heatedly caught up in the weaving contest: Minerva, who descended to earth disguised as an old crone, and the youthful, confident Arachne, one of the nine daughters of King Pieros, each of whom was foolish enough to challenge the muses or gods to a match of skill. The everyday world is thus shot through at every level with surprising correspondences and multiform changes. This dialogical trajectory from familiar to unfamiliar and then back again also cuts through the depth of the picture. The small, luminous interior suspended in the back presents the gossamer vision of an alien realm that demands to be coordinated with the shadowy frame of the larger surrounding scene in which it is epiphanically embedded.

The *Spinners* is a double provocation: it simultaneously elevates and deflates. Velásquez challenges contemporary artisans to spin like the gods, yet the *technē* of myth seems no different from the craft practiced by human beings. Recall that even after close inspection, no flaw could be detected in Arachne's cloth so that Minerva, in frustration, struck her forehead with a spindle, metamorphosing the upstart girl into a spider dangling in midair. But it was the magic of Velásquez's mimetic art that made such category-defying alterations of physical shape possible through the painterly interlace of spatial with temporal dimensions.

While there was considerable fluidity, even confusion, between analogical and allegorical procedures from antiquity though the early modern period, the intensification of the exclusively allegorical tradition occurred with the romantics. Kant's analysis of the Sublime in the *Critique of Judgment* (1790) prepared the ground for this insurmountable division. At one blow, he snapped the long Aristotelian line of thought—continuing through Hume, Hartley, and Reynolds—holding that the corporeal and incorporeal domains mutually illuminated one another. In his witty ultimate discourse, the "Discourse to Posterity," Sir Joshua Reynolds spoke movingly of "trying to reconcile contradictories, that of individualism, imagination and associative values with that of uniformity, reason and ideal form." His portraiture embodied this "amalgam of degree." According to the President of the Royal Academy, "individualism and ideal form are rather a difference of degree than of kind and we might be grateful for their presence now and in the future; perhaps presence matters more than degree." His subversive observation that, in his day, high society modeled itself after his pictures—"but how will a society which does not model itself after my work model itself and thus, see my painting in another modality"—gets at the heart of the relationship between past and future, the available and the unavailable. In an act of analogical affirmation, Reynolds predicts that, just as happened with Rembrandt, Rubens, Raphael, and Michelangelo, posterity will see "what has not yet been seen in my painting by my society."[25]

This "something else" that makes its eventual appearance, as if embedded in the work yet answering to the expectations of a different time, is beauty's power to forge allusive connections. While Reynolds's contemporary, Kant, deemed the Beautiful capable of relating the sensible to the intelligible sphere, he assigned greater weight and superiority to the Sublime. In the Sublime, the analogy between man and nature is made only to be broken, since it alone is absolutely great or "great beyond all comparison."[26] Sublimity underscored the isolation of the *Ding-an-sich*, that incommensurable thing that cannot be known as it is known or appears to itself.[27] Kant's heroization of the dynamic confrontation of the faculties of the mind, in the third *Critique* (1790), overturned the ideal of their unifying interaction to glorify discordant accord.[28] Not only did this internal tug of war derealize the aesthetic object, but the pleasure resulting from this failure to achieve accord was negative.

When the subject faced the nonrepresentable colossal heights and terrifying abysses of the Sublime, her aesthetic judgment was incapable of drawing affinities because of the excesses of the object and the inadequacies of the imagination. The resulting turmoil of reason and deregulation of the senses tormented Goya to Rimbaud. From the early *Caprichos* (1799) to the late murals decorating the dining room in the "House of the Deaf Man" (1819–1823), made to be activated with the piercing beam from a magic lantern, Goya recorded the pessimistic breakdown of the Enlightenment's

48. Francisco de Goya, *Aquelarre (The Great Goat)*, 1819–1823.

progressive belief in the force of intelligence. Only imbecilities and foibles emerged when one confronted the actuality of an empirical world left to its own superstitious devices (fig. 48). By brusquely inlaying spots of light with prevailing darkness, Goya's aquatinted and painted visions demonstrated the powerlessness of the unmoored intellect to unify a monstrously hybrid experience according to its own a priori transcendental laws.[29]

The exaggerated critical attention paid to the oppositional Sublime at the expense of the affinity-generating Beautiful—from Schlegel to Bataille—has skewed aesthetic and moral theory. The chaotic, the ugly, the literally repellent, or distance-producing, has been extolled, while the harmonizing aspect of subjectively experienced pleasure has been shunted to the side.[30] Nonmimetic allegory unseated mimesis. While Kant's first two critiques at least held open the possibility of tying together pure with practical reason, the invocation of the disorderly Sublime rendered any connection between a supposedly rational being and manifold reality deeply problematic.[31]

If the fragment, aphorism, ruin, grotesque, and other shattered forms characterize allegorical compositions, then spinning, plaiting, and weaving capture the simultaneity of contraries, the permeability and elasticity of intersubjective reciprocity. The analogical universe, like our membraned body, is knit together. It resembles a Möbius strip, a continuous one-sided surface, investigated by topology, the mathematical study of geometric forms that do not change despite bending or stretching. From Ariadne's spool of unfurling string, to Plato's statesman braiding contradictory elements into a harmonious social *logos*, to the maze of the Internet, fragile fibers twist physical phenomena with intangible desires. Strikingly, hypermedia, that electronic database storage and retrieval mechanism developed to emulate the energy of human cognitive processes,[32] is based on a nonlinear structure that operates by encouraging the swift interlacing of interdependent ideas.

Such a collated and cross-connected cyberenvironment, much like Leibniz's integrated world vision of spiritual, intellectual, and political unity in diversity, characterizes the multimedia fission occurring in Sarah Krepp's loomed relief canvases. Colorful skeins and taut ribbons thread the cosmos in her bristling *White Noise* (1992), part of the *Endless Lists* series (fig. 49). The beholder is enticed to navigate through a complex semantic system with random entry points and intersecting trails. Krepp joins bits and pieces of communications systems. Braille, sheet music, esoteric texts, foreign languages, scientific and medical charts, X rays, computer papers, astrological figures, codes, maps, blueprints, grids, ruled measurements, and diagrams of dance steps densely link indecipherable with decipherable information, suturing the faraway to the near-at-hand. In Leibnizian fashion, legibility depends on the viewer's background and point of view. Pattern thus becomes synonymous with metaphysics. Ornamental twinings picture the myriad ways differentiated parts can coexist within a borderless whole.

Regina Frank's site-specific installation *Hermes' Mistress* (1995) also helps us envision *analogon* as the intersection of immanence with transcendence. She transforms an enveloping and monumentally scaled red velvet dress into a second skin or habitation. Long folds cascade down from Frank's limbs, widening outward into a public space, and then ripple upward again from the hem's circular edge to be gathered into the still center of the self.[33] Whether we think of Penelope's compulsive doing and undoing of her nuptial *pharos* (fig. 50), or the great cloak offered in Athens every four years to Athena Polias at the festival of the Great Panathenaea, or the MIT Media Lab's intelligent fabrics, textiles provide both literal and figurative references to our tensioned condition of being tangled within life's richly textured, all-over design.

Even more than the raveling and unraveling of cloth, Far Eastern calligraphy instantiates analogy's swift process of repetition and permutation,

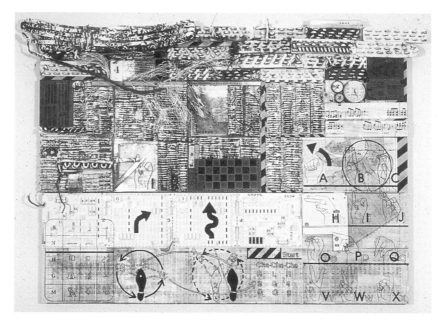

49. Sarah Krepp, *White Noise—Dancing in the Dark,* 1992.

visualized in Ed Moses's unfurled horizontal, scroll-like painting *Flight of Agents* (fig. 51). "Bisociation" was Arthur Koestler's term for this interlocking of two domains of knowledge previously believed unrelated or incompatible.[34] Chinese ideographs, in particular, permit us to see the dangers inherent in doubling, the *diabolon* lurking at the heart of *sumbolon*, the perils arising any time a cohesive "I" merges with a disruptive other.[35] The transformation of a generative into a destructive figurative process, I am suggesting, is akin to the historical turn away from analogy's combinatorial strategy to embrace allegory's reification of independent and unbridgeable modes of experience.

Two types of disorder threaten the intertwining of identity with alterity: confusion and discontinuity. When compound characters break apart, the remaining fragments are liable to mate helter-skelter with any neighboring element, and so lose their unitary meaning in an incompre-

50. Joseph Wright of Derby, *Penelope Unravelling Her Web,* 1783–1784.

51. Ed Moses, *Flight of Agents,* 1993.

hensible welter. Confusion also emerges when the internal alignment goes awry and the various components drift unmoored, severing the connection between text and speech, sign and signifier. Discontinuity, specifically, arises when these atomistic particles regain their absolute, if contextless, autonomy and stand radically divided from the rest of the discourse.[36]

This fundamental problem of determining the proper relation of parts to a whole—whether in a text, picture, or society—inspired the development of analogy in the first place. At its origin is the vision of a magically maintained cosmic harmony, which systematic philosophers later attempted to codify in intellectual constructs like participation or predication. The example of Chinese pictographs speaks to the difficulties of establishing and evaluating relationships, whether between actual things or between their representations. To control the profusion of characters and produce order, two requirements must be satisfied. An immediately perceived distinctness or unity of its own must be conferred on each character to rule out the chances for confusion. At the same time, each unit must possess properties enabling it to become a link in a semantic chain and so avoid a dramatic rupture with what went before. To express something new, then, means that each character must simultaneously maintain, while overstepping, traditionally established boundaries.

Vision is thus central to understanding how parts and wholes hang together. From the pre-Socratics to Leibniz, it was by dint of looking at things that we could feel our way back into their invisible core. Human beings projected life into objects, but, as in Epicurean extramissionist optics, objects also unpeeled their filmy species and sent these diaphanous apparitions back to reenter the beholder's eyes and consciousness.[37] In thrall to their mutual fascination, both viewer and viewed shared in the genesis of the world. Imagine this multifaceted exchange as taking place between two separate electronic interfaces operating in distant locations and transmitting live video images to one other. The recombined monadic image, as in Paul Sermon's alarmingly real installation *Telematic Dreaming* (1995), functions like a mirror that reflects one person within another person's reflection.[38]

In order to bring these rhetorical and philosophical concepts to life, I have tried to show the practices of "the relational way" enacted in works of art. But we need to recast the issue in technical terms as well. I want now to demonstrate how analogy moved from being an affirmative dialectics, an intelligent optimism following the *via eminentiae*, to become caught in the trammels of the *via negationis*. Allegory emerges when there is no hope that a compelling similarity might be established, or even pursued. It revels in paradox and spurns the coordination of asymmetric situations.[39]

Historically, there were two distinctive, yet not always easily kept separate, conceptions of analogy. These fueled acrimonious metaphysical, theological, and epistemological debates. The first was concerned with fixing the amount or *proportion* of the One that could also be *predicated* of the many. This position was stated by Thomas Aquinas (c. 1225–1274) as the *similitudo duarum ad invicem proportionum* and the *unius ad alterum*.[40] The second involved recognizing the *likeness* in name, or similarity of appearance, in which two unlike entities *participated*.[41]

The former, or mathematical, view ultimately stemmed from Parmenides (sixth century B.C.). In his poem on truth (or *Nature*), beauty, or the One, true Being, must be changeless, homogeneous, consistent, i.e., "autonomous and explainable in its own terms, a perfect, unified self-subsistent Whole."[42] Since it was forbidden to mix categories and the One was by nature permanent, the tie between incongruent realms had to be formal or abstract. Multiple and mutable beings could have only a numerical relation to that elevated Supreme Being which generated them. Pythagoras subsequently worked out quasi-mystical *paradeigmata*, that is, intervening mathematical formulae or geometrical outlines, to establish the *ratio propria* of plural individuals to a superior invisible presence.

In her wonderful invention of the asthmatic *savant* Marcus Potter, in *The Virgin in the Garden* (1978), A. S. Byatt conjures up what it is like to survey things proportionally, from no vantage, or all at once. Playing a game called "spreading, " the young mathematical genius "had to teach himself to find his body by shrinking his attention until it was momentarily located in one solid object." From such points, he could "in some spyglass way" search out his cold, crouching self and "with luck leap the mud across to it." It was geometry that afforded the grip and passage in ways that the sodden fields around Bilge Pond did not. "Broken chalk lines, the demarcation of winter games crossing summer ones, circles, parallel tram lines, fixed points, mapping out the surging, swimming mud, held it under, were lines to creep along, a network of salvation."[43] Marcus teeters between two opposing, Neoplatonist-inspired heresies. He is torn between pantheism, imagining that he is in some sense "spread out" through the immensity of the material universe, and Manicheanism, dualistically denying that an infinite God of light is in the perishable body or in the plants and stones of an evil world.[44]

In subsequent centuries the Parmenidean tradition, as Byatt's sympathetic portrait shows, led to a radical transcendentalism unwilling to reconcile the suffering of this life with the notion of a just and benevolent divinity. Human identity was dichotomized and decorporealized, with spirit wrenched from its domicile. The view that souls emanate eternally from God, like sunlight from the sun, favors a backward-moving, formal logic of generation divorced from incarnation. During the Middle Ages, heated arguments between Catholics and Cathars, in particular, raged over the question of the nature of the connection possible between an immutable, indivisible God and his divisible creation. To counter the heretical depreciation of the flesh and the invocation of an infinite distance between sin and grace, John Duns Scotus (1266–1308) attempted to spiritualize physical phenomena without either confusing them with God or drastically severing them from Him.

This formidable anti-Thomist devised an abstractive metaphysics—using the geometry of his opponents—to try to solve the theological difficulty of how plural, finite beings could be conjoined with a monistic, infinite Creator. The Franciscan *doctor subtilis* argued that material things and the eternal One are essentially, if only diagrammatically, connected. He demonstrated this thesis by considering the formal ratio of a suggested predicate (for example, *wise*), and then removing all limitations and imperfections from it. The precise subtraction of substance, like Marcus Potter's reduction of topographical features to nonmimetic schemata, permits us to assign the minimalist remainder to an immaterial divinity.[45]

From the thirteenth-century Neoplatonist Ramon Llull's logical "Art," based on pasting letters of the alphabet on revolving wheels to create mathematical permutations on the Divine Names and Attributes,[46] to the seventeenth-century Jesuit Athanasius Kircher's *Ars Magna Sciendi* and *Musurgia Universalis*, harmony emerged from ringing the changes on a set number of symbols. Even in Kircher's more applied investigations—such as his study of earthly and solar vulcanology—the underpinnings of the material universe remained sharply diagrammed. In this case, the triune relationship structuring the frontispiece to the *Mundus Subterraneus* (1678) was accentuated by compressing the cloud- and smoke-encircled globe—hovering between hellish underworld and shining firmament—into the center of an emblem-laden rectangular page (fig. 52).

At this point I want to alter course to take up the participatory theory of analogy celebrated in Plato's light-shot cosmology. In the *Timaeus* (29–30) and the *Republic* (472 b–e), he developed the notion of an image's sharing or partaking in a pattern, although this exemplification occurred in a static or unequal way. Moreover, it is through intuition or beholding that we come to know what is innate. Insight allows us to infer the ontological and phenomenological likeness binding seemingly unrelated structures.[47] Both a metaphysics and a logic, a vision and a form of reasoning, this type of analogy paradoxically treats being as immediacy and as discursivity. Aristotle and Aquinas wrestled with the degrees of resemblance connecting that which was temporally and ontologically a posteriori to the a priori, existing before and above it. But the Neoplatonists, especially, delighted in multiplying shape-changing emanations and transparent apparitions floating enticingly between the composite world of substance and a unique, radiant cause.

Again, Byatt's heliotropic evocation of Marcus Potter's special gifts of consciousness is apt for analogy's *enargeia*, where the image is so vivid as to appear directly before the eyes. The boy tells his teacher, Lucas Simmonds, of his oracular *vision* of mathematics into which one must be initiated. "Well—I used to see—to imagine—a place. A kind of garden. And the forms, the mathematical *forms*, were about in the landscape and you would let the problem loose in the landscape and it would wander amongst the forms—leaving luminous trails. And then I saw the answer." Earlier in the story, under the pressure of his father's relentless interrogation, he had broken down at this juncture. But with gentle prodding, Simmonds gets him to continue:

You see—it was important to see only obliquely—out of the edge of the eye—in the head, the *kind* of thing it was, the area it was in, but never to look directly, to look away on purpose, and wait for it to rise to form. When you'd waited, and it was *there* in its idea, you could draw the figure or even say words to go with it. But it mustn't be fixed, or held down, or it . . . It was important to *wait*, and they, the people asking were pressing on me, how could I be patient, how could I, so I tried to fix, to fix, to fix . . . And it was no good.[48]

52. Athanasius Kircher, title page from *Mundus Subterraneus*, 1678.

This almost aquatic sensing of Ideal forms is akin to watching James Turrell's light projection, *Tolbyn* (fig. 53). The halo of bluish quartz halogen light blurs the geometry of the brilliant column. The hard edges liquefy the more the viewer tries to grasp its contours. Ellsworth Kelly's Platonic fascination with straight lines and arcs, gigantic monochromatic slabs and fans that appear to swim magically in space, is also less about objects and more about "curves" that exist only in calculated relationships with one another. These pictures make the walls vibrate in the almost hallucinatory clarity of their high-keyed and even chromatics.

More recently, Ed Ruscha's epiphanic *Picture without Words*, commissioned for the opening of the Getty Center, hovers above the glazed lobby of the Harold M. Williams Auditorium (fig. 54). Although hanging inside Richard Meier's stunning crystal palace, it still manages to evoke an otherworldly presence by the diaphanous projection of a gigantic beacon. The towering 23-foot-high oil painting captures subtly striated white light theatrically cutting through a black ground as if entering from a high window. The ray falls at a raking slant to form a rectangular patch on the floor. The pronounced contrast between brilliance and tenebrousness causes the image to pulse like an emanation.

This metamorphic effect of subtle and continual irradiated motion also occurs in miniature. Reminiscent of Anne Hyde's small pop-up mirror poem—reflecting a French word on the left contour of a sliced paper disk in an English term on the right (fig. 55)—Kelly's parallelograms ripple and swell with the expansion or contraction of the gallery interior just as Ruscha's bundled beam appears to drift and billow the longer one gazes into it. Kelly's great weightless monuments, like the *Three Panels: Orange Dark Gray Green*, also waver against the wall, turning its blankness into a swaying canvas on which the artist joyfully disposes his eccentrically cut single-color shapes.[49] These meteoric artifacts—along with Dan Flavin's numinous neon tubes or Jeff Wall's incandescent boxes—give off an auratic glow connecting the secret life of objects to the wider universe. Fundamentally, they are about the undoing of the rigidity of things, the Neoplatonic unfreezing of petrified categories through transformation.

It is not surprising that Byatt, whose unfinished Oxford doctoral dissertation (directed by Helen Gardner) was on Neoplatonic creation myths, is superb in describing the silent, sensuous contemplation without verbal accompaniment elicited by such photogenic works.[50] Theurgic Neoplaton-

53. James Turrell, *Tolbyn,* 1967.

ism's spiritualized geometry, the Gnostic awareness of the twoness of reality, and the Tantric world of Hindu mysticism, all invoke a type of gnosis in which the seer realizes that the luminous godhead alone exists and that all else is illusory. Ramakrishna, the famous nineteenth-century Bengali mystic, gives a light-struck account—akin to Marcus's epiphany—of his first vision of the black goddess, the divine mother, Kali.

It was as if the room, the door, the temple itself, everything vanished—as if there was nothing anywhere! And what was it that I saw? A boundless, endless, conscious ocean of light! Wherever and however far I looked, from all four directions its brilliant row of waves were roaring towards me . . .[51]

This almost delirious wonderment of the adept is typical of another Byatt character's experience of art. A black and white photograph of Rodin's *Danaïde* spurs the playwright, Alexander Wedderburn, to silently retrace the recumbent half-moon of the woman's spine. He also wordlessly fingers the miniature cairn of Barbara Hepworthesque stones, mounded on a shelf in

54. Ed Ruscha, *Picture without Words*, 1997.

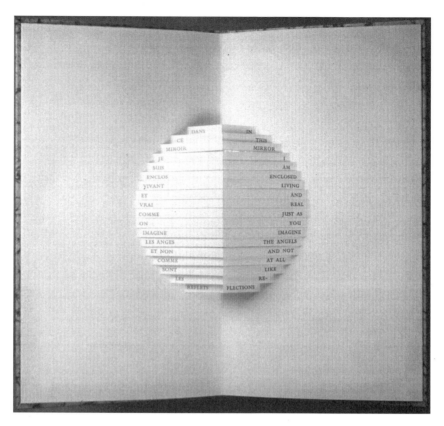

55. Anne Hyde, *Mirror (Artist's Book)*, 20th century.

his room, that taper into an arabesque of agate and alabaster menhirs.[52]

As Schopenhauer claimed in *The World as Will and Representation* (1819), aesthetic contemplation lies beyond description and induces silencing.[53] The exalted self's liberation from his individual will—like the Buddha's blissful state of nirvana—suppresses subjectivity and enhances pure perception. Yet this passive, objective perception of Platonic Ideas—reminiscent of the Hindu mysticism on which Schopenhauer draws—is deeply antianalogical. He shares with the later Neoplatonists, Gnostics, and the post-Kantian romantics the lack of interest in the immediate perception of the ordinary world where we encounter things in their instrumental relations as opposed to their nonfunctional essences. For Schopenhauer, the key to salvation lies in accurately viewing and correctly understanding what one has seen. Yet where is one to locate the deciphering guide in possession of hyperknowledge, without whom the beholder is doomed to wander among enigmas and riddles and so miss the true path?

Reason thus sits dangerously near unreason when the seer is autistically absorbed in his vision or lacks the hermeneutic key to esoteric knowledge. For Plato, and especially the hallucinatory late Neoplatonists, knowing is insight, an exalted discrimination. There are no sharp divisions separating an individual from that which precedes it. Something is true only by virtue of the Idea of Truth which lesser, particular truths mirror inadequately. Nor is the One identical with any of its manifestations, yet they all participate unequally in the same Reality. Without discerning a kinship between inquirer and object, Plato argued, it was impossible to discover affinities.[54] But as the binding process became allegorized—that is, as the subject became almost preternaturally aware of the discontinuities abruptly severing the world as it appears in the mind as idea from the world existing outside of thought—making connections became increasingly arbitrary.

If, for Schopenhauer, the loss of self-consciousness in aesthetic contemplation meant that we cease to be aware of the spatial, temporal, and causal relations in which we stand to the object,[55] for Hegel it meant achieving a kind of redemptive final restoration of unity. The transcendental circularity of Hegel's *Vernunft*, which miraculously "lifts up" every difference of thought or being and synthesizes these deficiencies in a more perfect third term, leads to dialectic identity.[56] His idealist philosophy represents a late and systematic reprise of earlier symbolic practices intent on dissolving the binary categories constructed by society. The acutely perceiving subject has the power to rise above and transform a passive reality awaiting instantiation by the discovery and creation of doubling images or manifesting correspondences. Despite their differences, both Hegel's and Schopenhauer's contemplated object passes either out of the reach of our will or beyond mimesis into a nonrepresentational knowledge for which nonprogrammatic music stands as the highest incarnation.

3

The Magic of
Amorous Attraction

In other words, after Chaos, the Earth and Love, these two came into being. Also Parmenides sings of Generation: "First in the train of gods, he fashioned Love."
Plato, Symposium

Something fundamental happened to the concept of unity with the advent of the romantics. But this revolutionary shift from a woven coherence (as in the intertwining of sexually dissimilar threads)[1] to a granular world order ultimately derived from a late antique seismic shock. Under the pressure of a militantly monotheistic Christianity, the promiscuous syncretism (at its height between 250 and 350 A.D.) propagated throughout the Roman Empire from the great pluralizing cult centers of Asia Minor was replaced during the course of the next two centuries by a single abstinent and antimaterialist cult.[2]

On one hand, after much struggle the hybrid deities projected through the optical technology of Egyptian and Syrian temple magic were unseated by a universalizing Church whose obscure typologies and esoteric parallelisms could never adequately meet in this life. Ironically, on the other hand, early Christianity—so eager to establish its difference from the "oriental" heterodoxy threatening to engulf it—itself lapsed into multiplying heresies, secret exegesis, and mysterious rituals. Witness the explosion of the great ecumenical councils attempting to distill doctrinal purity out of a welter of errancy: Nicaea in 325, Constantinople in 381, Ephesus in 431, and Chalcedon in 451.[3]

The disintegrating Alexandrian school, composed of the combined rival influences of Platonism, Aristotelianism, and Neoplatonism, mixed its debris with the newer ruins of imperial Rome's assaulted cults, with Manicheanism, Mithraism, Zoroastrianism, and Gnosticism, further spiced by the dark paradoxes of Philo, Apollonius of Tyana, and the Pseudo-Dionysius. This massive shattering of a holistic cultural vision grounded in a shared theology left weird progeny and enigmatic "intelligences"[4] in its lengthening wake.

There is an old linkage between sex and religion. Occult relations are basically about joining or fusing or being penetrated by some superior being. One aspect of the slow slide from an analogical into an allegorical universe was that the world's geography was increasingly and unswervingly made to point toward a metaphysical topography. To avoid sinking into the quagmire of hermeticism, I will be using Gnosticism to explore one of a series of similar displacements away from an "infectious" universe in thrall to coupling forces, toward one in bondage to divorcing vertical and horizontal vectors. In place of more robust perceptual encounters between an individual psyche and the cosmos, Gnosticism offered the blissful sensing, at once chaste and fleshy, of the invisible aura of the holy. Where analogy dissolved hierarchical divisions through an interwoven combinatorics, allegory mechanically reproduced an infinity of steps on a receding ladder to be ascended or descended by the initiate.

The analogical vision of a superabundant yet indescribable One flowing into all creation shored up an eroticized theory of correspondences. Contagious or homeopathic magic initially developed because the influence of like upon like was rarely clear. Physiognomics, chiromancy, dream interpretation or oneirocriticism, omen-ridden astrology, and alchemy all required an exegetic unfolding of implicit meaning from explicit signs (fig. 56). This drama of interpretive longing can be called "genetic criticism."[5] The begetting of the work of art and the desire to divine its original significance were thus connected to the bodily impulse to procreate and to the physiological functions of gestation and childbearing, resulting in offspring and, more abstractly, in a cosmological order founded on filiation (fig. 57).[6] But the family of concentric circles and intimately nested spheres of the Ptolemaic universe stood in stark contrast to the isolation of human beings from a remote divinity reified in the Copernican scheme. The modern scientific specimen, in this case a preserved fetus, visually embodies such extreme distancing from an infinite God (fig. 58). Even when the preparation was recomposed into an elaborate allegorical *vanitas*, as occurred in the macabre medical collection contrived by the Dutch anatomist Frederick Ruysch (fig. 59), man was excised from an animate universe and abruptly relocated within the limited human moral order.

Eros and Anteros, love and its opposite, lay at the heart of any quest that went beyond reason. The pursuit of the unknown mirrored the ardor of carnal desire; its charged language of sympathy and antipathy evoked the amorous attraction magnetizing a pair of lovers. It was believed by alchemists and theosophists that analogy could acquaint us with the hidden source of that hypnotic power which inexplicably attracted and repelled us. From Gnostic attempts to make the soul tangible as a whore or virgin, to heretical discussions of the three diverging genders of the Nicene Trinity,[7]

56. Stefan Michelspacher, *End [of the Alchemical Great Work]: Multiplication,* 1663.

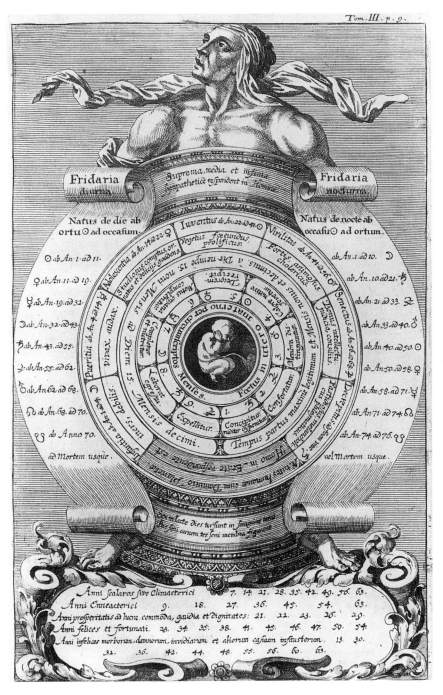

57. Johann Zahn, *Human Conception,* 1696.

58. Frederick Ruysch, *Lower Jaw with Teeth
Preserved in a Jar, Microscopic Enlargement of
a Section of a Cheek, Fetus in Amniotic Sack,*
1715.

59. Frederick Ruysch, *Vanitas Assemblage,* 1703.

analogy's transcategorical terms offered a way to talk about an ineffable divinity that could be approached alternately only by stages or by total immersion. By extension, its branching and ramifying imagery provided figures of comparison for all complex experiences that were in process and eluded words. Needless to say, systematic philosophy had difficulties with this cosmic love affair because of its contradictory and spontaneous tendency to communicate messages on many levels and, at the same time, its refusal to communicate them.

In this chapter I will be looking at four moments in the career of analogy as an erotic-religious force. First, I outline the ways in which the pre-Socratics down through Plato devised rhetorical techniques for marrying the familiar with the unfamiliar. Second, I show through a case study in allegorizing theurgy, the Gnostic romance of *Chaereas and Callirhoe*, how these earlier conjugal weavings unraveled in irrational ways and became the subject of a High Enlightenment critique of fanatical "eclecticism." Third, I incorporate Aristotle and his distinguished medieval follower Aquinas into what, so far, has been a predominantly Neoplatonic trajectory. My purpose in recuperating this alternative analogical tradition is to expose the long shadow cast by the *analogia entis* debates in Catholic and Protestant theology well into the twentieth century. Finally, I argue that Leibniz was the last great "amatory" philosopher of the modern period to use analogy without inverting it into the negative dialectics of allegory. In his hands, it once again became a combinatorial method for coordinating myriad human institutions requiring new "attachments," innovative types of concentrated interconnected information.

Long before E. O. Wilson's theory of consilience and without the latter's hierarchical reductivism,[8] Leibniz argued for a nuanced, yet encyclopedic, type of synthesis to heal the fragmentation of knowledge and belief that had arisen in the early modern period among competing interpretive groups. In addition, his metaphysics and epistemology prepared the conceptual ground for thinking about the sociotechnical and the visual-verbal implications of digital convergence. As I argued in *Good Looking*, we are witnessing the simultaneous explosion of omnimedia and the funneling of all preexisting media and content into a single virtual multimedium though the global, decentered, and highly integrated Net. In light of this compressive drive affecting all areas of our culture, it is important to see that the kind of analogical knitting together Leibniz proposed avoids Wilson's isomorphic program for intellectual annexation, whereby one branch of learning is subsumed under a more "fundamental" or powerful science. Leibniz's ontology and his aesthetics, taken together, form one massive nonreductive associative program hyperlinking the personal to the suprapersonal.

This mediation with the divine world through a tangible link was an innovation of the pre-Socratics. They initiated the metaphorical process of going beyond the limits of actual knowledge to seize a tantalizing, but foreign, reality. In Paul Grenet's words, the preclassical Greeks adopted an "analogical attitude"[9] to cope with the problem of how to depict the existence of what cannot be seen, such as a separate soul, or to suggest the idea of an ephemeral substance without a body. Wind, smoke, shadow, dream, fire, and image were the phenomenological terms of comparison they borrowed to marry the suprasensible to the sensible realm. Homer and Hesiod used personification to wed quarrels happening atop Mount Olympus to battles raging below at Troy.

But it was Heraclitus (536–470 B.C.), the greatest of the Ionians, who turned analogy away from simple, vertical anthropomorphism and honed it into a general tool for scientific explanation. His concept of nature riven by war applied equally to the experimental areas of chemistry, biology, law, ethics, and affairs of the heart. Discord or concord are possible within any mixture compounded of contraries. The fires and forges so dear to him—like those depicted in a Wright of Derby painting—revealed the violent struggle that preceded any integration or renovation of opposites.[10] It is not accidental that Heidegger, who modeled his distinction between Being and being on Heraclitus, saw the relationship between conflict and harmony as leading to the redemption of a philosophy of difference.[11] Following in his footsteps, Foucault coined the term "arthrology" for a science of the "joints" between forms of discourse within an overall epistemological configuration. These common tropes lie below the surface and must be unearthed through comparison.[12]

Empedocles expanded the associative/dissociative tendencies in Heraclitus's principle of change and further transformed them into dehumanized drives. Love and Strife depersonalized celestial mechanics into rhythmic impulsions imparting motion to the four elements. The implicit tension between the invisible springs and their visible effects—now sublimed into an enigmatic network of forces—was made explicit by Anaxagoras and Democritus. The physiognomic dictum asserting that what appears at the core of experience is a vision of what does not appear[13] was absorbed, in turn, by Plato (427–347 B.C.), who amplified these dichotomies through the addition of a mediator.

The dialectics of love, making it possible to analogize from the evident to the inevident, constitutes the central philosophical myth of the *Timaeus* and the *Symposium*. The Creator or Demiurge always stands in between thought and a more precious concealed Reality. In the *Phaedo*, *Parmenides*, and *Statesman*, logoi embody the analogical notion that conceptual representations, or images, enable us to make the transition from sensible things to otherwise unseizable intelligible Forms. These logoi are like mirroring water in which astronomers observe eclipses.[14] Distorted reflection and immutable Intelligence meet and mingle within a gently undulating medium, much as Raphael's crisply delineated fishermen in the tapestry cartoon of *The Miraculous Draft of Fishes* dissolve into a subtly diversified unity within the waves of the lake of Gennesaret (see fig. 14). Liquidity mediates the absolute opposition between any two incongruous orders—whether they be phenomena and noumena, body and soul, body and bodies—rendering their irreconcilability approximate, their resemblance verisimilar.

There is an important distinction to be drawn, then, between being antithetical and being inimical. The determinism of extreme dissent, arcing from Nietzschean nihilism to the poststructuralist and deconstructionist discourse of radical dissatisfaction,[15] continues to fuel the impoverished contemporary concept of the similar as the empty simulacrum. The Platonic theory of imitation through intervening logoi, on the contrary, can be mapped according to the sensuous geometry of the divided line, imaginatively cut by the sudden vaulting diagonal of analogy.

The Neoplatonists increasingly mathematized the intercourse between heaven and earth, sexualizing the propagation of numerous copies into multitudinous progeny. Their developmental vocabulary—transformed by later alchemists into the steps required to achieve the real and spiritual gold of the Great Work—derived from Plato's henological argument of hierarchical gradations (fig. 60).[16] To ascend from the composite to the simple, the many must participate by calculable degrees in the essence of the One. During this simultaneously arithmetical, mystical, and erotic journey upward, things tended progressively to submerge their own proper identity. As their physicality became increasingly "sublimed" into

60. Stefan Michelspacher, *Middle [of the Alchemical Great Work]: Conjunction,* 1663.

shadows, traces, sparks, or symbols of the highest Being, these distilled particles voluptuously drowned in the well of the ultimate divinity. Paradoxically, logical sequence was thus transformed into the instantaneous vision of Neoplatonic myth. A complex process that extended over a long period of time dramatically imploded. Marshall McLuhan found this contraction to be typical of a Hebraic or "Eastern" mode of thought. In these oral societies messages were traced and retraced on cylinder seals and on the concentric spirals of a column with seeming redundancy, to achieve sudden insight.[17]

Analogy as a method for *mediating*—i.e., maintaining a proportional or *balanced* relation—between the world of experience and the noetic realm thus vanished into the arabesque of equivocal allegory. The later Neoplatonists, Porphyry (233–305), Iamblichus (d. 330), and Proclus (412–485), in particular, failed to heed Plato's warning in the *Republic* (X.597e) about the dangers of incantatory illusion. This fantastic dream of union ignored the distinction between image and object; it never broke the lengthening trail of dependence even as the interval to be spanned diminished as one moved down the chain of being. Bonds became bondage maintained through spells. Qualities were not intrinsic to mutable appearances but consisted in their fixed, inverse schematic relation to an immutable God. Besotted by formulaic multiplications, the theurgic Neoplatonists either left no unfilled space or intervening medium in the universe in which the transactive leap to resemblance might take place or they left an untraversable chasm. The nominalist aspect of their doctrine held that only individual or disparate things existed; the essentialist side argued that our categories were absolute and unchanging. Such extremes could only be married allegorically, by the ironic location of a differential identity. As Proclus declared: "For it is the essence of symbolization to indicate the nature of what is real by what is most strongly antithetical to it. If, then, a poet is inspired and reveals by means of symbols the truth of existent things, such a poet is neither an imitator nor can he be proved wrong by empirical demonstrations."[18]

Before getting enmeshed in the multimodal intertwinings of late Neoplatonism with Gnosticism, it is worth pausing here for a moment to repeat some basic principles. Neither the anomalism[19] of divinatory allegory nor the endless interpretation of hermeneutics (which has its precedent in allegorical exegesis since it refuses to assign any truth value to the common sense) may be considered mere variants of the analogical principle of comparison. In analogy, resemblance is first and foremost a matter of mimesis, of clothing, rather than veiling, ideas. This impulse became obscured in the iconological tradition—continually anthologized from Ripa to Boudard—that thrived on manufacturing puzzling emblems for abstract notions. Consequently, clear or muddled thoughts might be conceived as a female figure possessing a head sprouting wings and stretching out a hand holding a tangled hank of hair (fig. 61). By contrast, the goal of analogical imitation was to create an emulation that avoided the blatantly "false" look of such bizarre rebuses. This partial likeness also differed from the kind of replicating isomorphism we have grown accustomed to witnessing in contemporary advertisements. Warhol-inspired artists abandoned analogy not in favor of abstruse allegory, but to mock the tautological repetition of already mass-produced standard items (fig. 62).[20]

Among the later Neoplatonists, an irrationalist theurgy quickly insinuated itself into heresy-laced Gnosticism. Heterodoxy bloomed, but was obliged to hide in the Egyptian desert, during the founding days of orthodox Christian monasticism. These odd sects, with their privileged initiates, believed themselves to be participating directly in eternity and thus did not acknowledge a historical mediator like Jesus. The Christian Gnostics, from evidence in the Nag Hammadi manuscripts (late fourth century), radically sexualized and mystified the Neoplatonic genetic-obstetric process of emanation. In the occult tradition, gross materiality is a product of the Fall. This primal swerve away from monism, or Oneness, was reenacted in the Neoplatonic process of emanation. The descent of the soul (its painful "birth") from the ether to earth became further complicated and convoluted in the hermetic tradition. The spiritual body—that subtle, astral substance, or mediating "vehicle" enveloping the corporeal body and floating in between it and the fiery aerial spirit—became besmirched as it left the luminous firmament and touched the elementary darkness of the phenomenal world.

Gnostic texts, in particular, constructed an extreme opposition between the beauty, transparency, and androgyny of the prelapsarian body and its corrupt counterpart in this world. They also distinguished between pure, mental conception and lustful procreation. Physical reproduction even tainted certain divinities who gradually mingled with and became infected by the brutish elements of the lower realm. These demigods and

61. J. B. Boudard, *Thoughts,* 1766.

62. Charles Ray, *Bath,* 1989.

fallen angels begat a fantastic host of hypostatized figures. Recall that the Creation, as recounted in the book of Genesis, conjured up the image of a virile and palpable Jehovah who inspired analogous personifications of male potency (fig. 63).

"Archons," "Zoe," and "the Power of Sophia"[21]—depicted in the Manichean dramas of William Blake—were contradictory spiritual, psychic, and material energies that became incarnated in human form. Blake's Urizen was a bestial descendant of that Satanic "Aeon" who possessed and defiled the pneumatic Eve, Adam's "co-likeness" before the Fall. The dominion of the elemental world over Urizen was visualized in his filthy hirsute condition, the crusting over of his genitals, and the encasing of his original ethereal body in deformity. Blake's obsession with issues of likeness and difference in his biblical typological narratives (*The Marriage of Heaven and Hell, The Book of Urizen, Jerusalem*) was also uncannily reflected in his technical language as a virulently *non*reproductive engraver.[22] The struggle between type, prototype, and stereotype, in the artistic domain, mimicked the somatic consequences of the Fall.

In preclassical Greece, combat, friendship, betrothal, and childbirth had offered philosophers a way of representing abstract cosmic functions through concrete social ties. But in Gnosticism, everyday examples of parturition and growth became monstrous hybrids, personifications run wild. Events were black or white; guilt and sin were insuperable contraries without a point of contact.

Elaine Pagels, in her illuminating study of feminine imagery in the Gospel of Philip and other apocryphal writings like the Book of John, Daniel, or Baruch (avidly read by the romantics), emphasized Gnosticism's hermeneutic approach.[23] What is significant for our purposes is how the Gnostic *pneumatikoi*'s negative attitude toward marriage and procreation as a kind of pollution[24] *allegorized* as impure the very biblical passage that had been paradigmatic of *analogical* procedure, namely, that "two shall become one flesh" to produce offspring.[25] For the Gnostics, Adam's ideal, intimate union with Eve symbolized the harmony or fullness (*pleroma*) between the soul and an indwelling spirit. As Wisdom, she came from the world above in the guise of his restorative counterimage (*syzygos*). This alchemical transmutation of our first parents into ghostly partners served as an allegory of the Gnostic Christian who, while imprisoned in his body,

63. Johann Zahn, *Verbo Domini,* 1696.

was roused by "the thought of the virginal spirit" (Apocalypse of John 30:32–31:22).[26]

Not only did carnality bear a direct but antithetical relation to spirituality, but likeness literally became isomorphism. The reunion of separated halves in "perfect marriage" applied to a spiritual, not a physical, Eve who was identical to Adam because, originally, she had been preformed or concealed within his soul. Conversely, I want to argue that adultery—or illicit entanglement—functioned in this psychomachia as a parody of analogy's bonds. Eve's initial transgression was to couple with the serpent. Joining with the beast signified the soul's ensnarement by unlike matter, alienating it from the spirit and driving both of them into disjunctive sin.[27] This allegory alluded to the soiling of primal counterimages that could be healed only through the purifying sacraments. Baptism and the Holy Eucharist, in particular, spelled death to former commitments and birth to a new life.

Consequently, resurrection in the spirit was the result of a mysterious and inspired process. While many Christian Gnostics of the fourth century balked at the idea that God could have entered the human sphere as a helpless infant born of a woman's body, others evoked Eve in positive religious symbols.[28] Analogy, too, stood both for lust and for the sacrament of marriage, fostering the resurrection not just of the soul but of the flesh as well. Similarly, we can detect its holistic operations in the Valentinian Christians' rejection of asceticism and their consecration of the entire person instead. According to Pagels, the Valentinians were enjoined to enact marital intercourse in ways that expressed the couple's spiritual, psychic, and bodily integration—itself symbolic of a greater pleromic harmony.[29]

The antithesis between prostitution and virginity also formed the stuff of Gnostic novels. Chariton's romance, the *Chaereas and Callirhoe* (from the middle of the first century A.D.)—significantly only discovered in 1750[30]—allegorized the soul's ardent, earthly trials in terms of violent passions played out against an eerie, preternatural, and cavernous interior. As Diderot intimated in his error-riddled ekphrasis of Fragonard's shadowy "Platonic" painting on the same subject (exhibited in the Salon of 1765), the theatrical romance involved the tragic separation of two lovers, a captured virgin, a temple priest, a tyrannical god, and an ecstatic reunion that was consummated in a frenzied, vapor-shrouded death (fig. 64).[31] Picture and story, as frequently happened in Diderot's poetic recastings,[32] do not precisely coincide. Inspired by Fragonard's steamy spectacle of eroticism

64. Jean-Honoré Fragonard, *Coresus and Callirhoe,*
Salon of 1765.

and orgiastic thaumaturgy at work, the Enlightenment *philosophe* went out
of his way to indict the superstition-mongering of an "Asiatic" priestcraft.
The sober details of the travel writer Pausanias's account of this same
story—a sanctuary dedicated to Dionysus containing his image brought
from Calydon, Coreseus, his priest, in love with a young girl, Callirhoe,
who does not return his affection, the wrath of the spurned lover, who
appeals to his god who then strikes the Calydonians mad, an oracle that
proclaims that the outbreak will cease only after Coreseus sacrifices his
beloved[33]—were reconstituted by the French writer into a veiled critique
of the superstitions of "eclecticism." I am suggesting, for the first time,
that Diderot's perplexing ekphrasis owed less to Pausanias's Baedekeresque
Description of Greece (150–180 A.D.), whose acknowledged intention was to
represent "all things Hellenic,"[34] and more to the *thaumata*-steeped rites

evoked in Chariton. Eclecticism, from the *Encyclopédie* article of the same name, was precisely the term bestowed by the Enlighteners on those "Gnostic" Neoplatonists who promoted irrationalism, magical operations, and obscene nocturnal performances.[35] Ancient wonders (*thaumata*) associated with strange sects uncomfortably resembled modern Rome's dubious miracles.

Uncannily, Fragonard's apparitional setting captures the doubleness of the Gnostic sacramental bedroom (*koiton*) or ritual intercourse, referred to in the Gospel of Philip,[36] whose secret activities supposedly heal the split between male and female, Adam and Eve. The androgyny of the priest Coresus, whose resemblance to Callirhoe was disparagingly remarked upon by Diderot, is a sign of the divided spirit's resuturing of her lower, worldly self to her upper, holy identity in the cult.[37] The bridal chamber ritual, prefigured in earthly nuptials, conveyed the message that dichotomies were illusory. As in Tantric mystico-erotic practices, nothing was impure because everything in the universe was composed of the substance of Vishnu.[38] Like the filmy smoke engulfing the interchangeable "puppets" in the painting, dualism dissolves into monism, light and darkness blend in a single revelation. Otherworldly mystery is indicated by a fleshy performance.

I want to set aside for a moment my theme—the conversion and inversion of harmonizing analogy into mystifying univocal allegory as operated by Neoplatonic and Gnostic magi—in order to look at the pragmatic Aristotelian formulation of the issue, which has had a long afterlife both in Western science and in Christian theology. For Aristotle (384–322 B.C.), analogy is both poetic and mathematical-philosophical. It belongs to the larger domain of metaphor, which, in turn, is a component of logic. "Translation" best describes its rhetorical function, since metaphor transports words from one order of reality to another.[39] Unlike the late antique allegorists we have been considering, Aristotle was more interested in discovering linkages than in divining riddling symbols from their empirical opposites.[40] Importantly, he imparted a specifically analogical twist to metaphor by formulating clear and precise accounts of poetic attribution. Aristotelian mimesis, or the activity of visibly converting and reconverting words in order to see phenomena in a new or better light, is fundamentally at odds with a negative, decoding hermeneutics.

In the *Topics*[41] and the *Prior Analytics*,[42] analogy is also discussed in terms of geometrical conformity and congruence, as Kant will later do when examining the operations of judgment.[43] As a type of incomplete induction enabling us to reason from the particular to the general, this act of comparison belonged to an art of discovery, not to a rigorous method. Francis Bacon (1561–1626), while brooding on how to bring about a complete renovation of the sciences (*instauratio magna*), elaborated on the inductive portion of Aristotle's discussion of analogy. Bacon's dream of the unity of knowledge—although far from the contemporary conception of it as the deliberate, systematic linkage of cause and effect across disciplines—has made him a hero to scientists such as E. O. Wilson who oppose professional atomization and the fragmentation of expertise.[44]

Although induction had been around for a long time, Bacon was unhappy with its ordinary speculative employment and ranked it among the illusions of the tribe (i.e., incorrect "anticipations" grounded in human nature and thus common to the whole race).[45] He demanded a more stringent induction, one that transcended the jumbled accumulation and simple enumeration typical of a merely anecdotal analogism. This ingenious stringing together of instances when a phenomenon occurred was to yield before a purified way of apprehending things in relation to themselves, to us, and to the universe at large. Experiments and the formulation of provisional hypotheses were expected to throw explanatory light on agreement and difference across a broad range of cases.

Invention, whether in poetics or logic, hinges on the creation of an equivocal middle term, one that literally stands in between the singular instance and the general rule. Similarity is the result of a complexly achieved identity, one that rises above each of the individual cases or terms to span items in different or distant categories. Because there are so many variables in bringing disparate properties together under a common rubric, resemblance is partial (i.e., equivocal), and the middle term in an Aristotelian syllogism always remains ambivalent.

Bacon clarified Aristotle's theory of induction, intensifying its arguments and crystallizing it into a system of abstraction: We require great masses of empirical data to extrapolate meaningful information and collate it correctly so as not to leap to premature conclusions. Thomas Aquinas, earlier, had laid the groundwork for Bacon's attempt at synthesis. In spite of science's division into separate branches, Aquinas stressed the participatory mechanisms undergirding any transition from the known to the unknown. The *Summa contra Gentiles* built upon Aristotle's claim that analogy offered a "mesothesis," or second term among three, to reflect upon, describe, and approach God. Unlike the Neoplatonists, St. Thomas allowed for reason's natural capacity to understand metaphysical reality by comparing it to the images that bore its likeness.

This positive relational perspective—putting human experience in mediated contact with the divine—was essentially optimistic. Aquinas's sensorial anthropology, holding out the promise of potential harmony between nature and grace, was thus distinct not only from Neoplatonic rituals like those of the Pseudo-Dionysius, conjuring the divine presence from where it was not, but also from Jewish Cabala, excavating truths from the mystifying names of Jehovah. His doctrine of the Beatific Vision—maintaining that the highest and perfect felicity of the intellect consists in the vision of God[46]—also differed from Augustine's (354–430) almost insuperable Manicheanism. The latter's uncompromising view, deepened and extended through the writings of saints Paul and Jerome, eventually became absorbed into the puritanical strains of post-Reformation Protestantism. Even when the spirit stripped off the body through grueling ascetic practices, the gulf opened by original sin remained untraversable. The soul's radical "nakedness," after baptism, was insufficient to reestablish the order of agreement that had existed between the uncreated essence and God's creation before the Fall.[47]

The transcendental hermeneutics of German idealism—spread by Coleridge—reopened the doctrinal battles of the Protestant Reformation centered around the interpretation of sacred scripture. It simultaneously rearticulated the quandary surrounding the relationship of the visible to a constantly withdrawing invisible realm. The recurring crisis is, once again, about whether one can put a material object or physical icon in relation to something that is disembodied, and what the nature of that resemblance is.[48] Is it that of a facsimile or of a purely formal identity, or of an approximating imitation of an absent prototype? In discussing the Eucharist, Martin Luther had defended the literal, consubstantiation sense of the statement *Hoc est corpus meum*, and opposed the Roman Catholic "analogical" dogma of the transubstantiation of Jesus's body and blood into the host. The Swiss reformer Ulrich Zwingli, however, understood the phrase entirely symbolically, that is, allegorically, in the special sense I have been developing. Basing his interpretation on the *est* portion of the statement, i.e., on the verb *is* which married two discrepant things (bread and body), he denied Luther's synecdochic identification of the two. Instead, bread and wine were merely an arbitrary "representation and a memorial" of Christ's body and blood.

The Supper, therefore, was not a participation in the "real presence" but only emblematic of it. Zwingli thus profoundly allegorized the Eucharist since faith alone, not the bodily eating, made it an efficacious rite. This robbed the sacrament of its incarnational reality and power as an actual means to attain grace. John Calvin argued, in line with Luther, that even though the symbol and thing differed in essence, the symbol truly exhibited it. The bread was not just an arbitrary token signifying Christ's body.[49] Yet, ultimately, Calvin questioned the ability of any human sign to represent or analogize God's infinite glory.

The Thomistic or Roman Catholic construction of *analogia entis* (the analogy of that which is), as located midway between pure univocation and pure equivocation, had affirmed that a likeness really existed between God and his creatures. Aquinas adopted the Aristotelian idea that when an agent produced an effect, it transmitted something of its own into the latter such that some likeness remained traceable from the effect to the cause.[50] In the twentieth century, Karl Barth, conversely, expanded on Augustine's mistrust of *theologia positiva*, asserting that to link the being of fallen humanity to the Supreme Being dialectically was the invention of the anti-Christ.[51] For the great Heideggerian theologian, the danger of making such a connection was that it demoted God to one of man's potential thoughts. For him, the only solution to such an intolerable predication was always to exclude or abstract imperfection from perfection. Paul Tillich, in turn, attempted to redress the extreme bent toward negative theology of the Barthian sort. He saw such skewing as a mirror of the crisis surfacing in Protestantism between the wars. Tillich criticized Barth for his radical monism, his positing of an enormous remoteness that reduced humanity to aliens and turned sin into something unreal—because unimaginable—and grace into an unattainable, and so irrational, aspiration.

The modern fracturing of the bond between creator and creation amplified Proclus's uncompromising view of allegory as the signification of the real by what was most antithetical to it. Importantly, Tillich attempted to offset the rigid Protestant division between mortal and immortal by erecting his theology on analogical equilibrium. The task of religion became the search for junctures potentially connecting immanence to transcendence. Influenced by Cusanus and Meister Eckhardt, he argued that mankind stood in a dual relationship to God. Our condition is simultaneously one of knowing and not-knowing.[52]

In 1963, the Czech Thomist Erich Przywara again brought the *analogia entis* question to the forefront of controversy. He maintained that it replayed the old opposition between Parmenides's assertion that Being was identity and Heraclitus's declaration that Being was difference. The Catholic theologian attempted to resolve the contemporary quandary by reviving Aristotle's two senses of analogy: as a predicate (all perfection belongs to God and belongs to his creations only secondarily) and as a proportion (establishing the ratio between unity and multiplicity). Przywara reclaimed this doubleness for analogy so as to argue that the One has the capacity to be diverse.[53]

A constant theme of metaphysics—from Augustine to Descartes to Barth—was the need to overcome resemblance. In one way or another, mimetic or analogical theories posited mirroring as central to their project, while allegoresis refused to reflect. For philosophy, as well as theology, the perils of imagination then consisted in following a chain of similarities that might lead us astray or seduce us into seeing erroneous connections.[54] For Nietzsche, it was only by an aphoristic refusal of plenitude that generation took place. For Heidegger, Being came into its own through painstaking differentiation from beings. For Benjamin, the decline of aura was commensurate with the melancholic interplay of nostalgia and loss.[55]

Against the backdrop of a rising tide of allegory, Gottfried Wilhelm Leibniz (1646–1716) emerges as the last of the visionary analogists. This celebrated philosopher, diplomat, mathematician, coinventor of the differential calculus, and all-around polymath deserves to be recognized as the heir of the Plato of the logoi, not of the demonology of the Neoplatonists. A major difficulty dogging a proper assessment of his fundamentally aesthetic system is that it remains eclipsed by the overestimation of Kant's critiques.

The encyclopedism of the late *Monadology* (1714)—a kind of cosmic pointillism coordinating an infinity of copresent individuals—took up the Scholastic challenge to connect God with man. Leibniz, however, transformed this medieval quest into a spatiotemporal game, a gigantic jigsaw puzzle bringing an infinite atomic diversity into compossible concordance. His simultaneously inductive and deductive system also possessed a commanding point of view lacking in Bacon's doctrine of the "idols"—the illusion that has each individual inhabiting a Platonic "cave" from whose opening she regards a universe in a peculiar and disconnected manner.

Resemblance was central to the baroque delight in paradox. Witty *coincinnitas*, defined by Thomas Browne as the union of "incompatible distances in some middle and participatory nature,"[56] meant that nothing was exclusively one thing or another. This playful combination of preexisting forms was also typical of the tiling that subdivided and unified the precious surfaces of a seventeenth-century *Kunstschrank* (fig. 65). Such wondrous chests, stocked with *artificialia, naturalia*, and *scientifica*, differed importantly from the church reliquaries that were their ancestors. No matter how elaborate the monstrances containing the flayed face of St. Bartholomew (fig. 66) or fragments of the fingers ripped from the hands of saints Zacharias, Jerome, and George (fig. 67), their pessimistic doctrinal and instructional ambition was not to cross-reference the universe. In the punitive hands of Lutheran reformers, the body parts of Christian martyrs—scarred with signs of mutilation, amputation, and execution—were stern instruments for psychological and pedagogical conditioning.[57] The brutal display of one or several tortured religious remains to inculcate disobedient children and recalcitrant adults in true Protestant faith took a very different tack in Counter-Reformation Catholic countries.

During the 1600s the Jesuits, especially, encouraged seriocomic gatherings of natural and artificial phenomena that were playfully and informatively ensconced in niches, drawers, chests, and eventually rooms. Spiraled nautilus shells and intricately turned ivories constituted an immanent science joining nature with culture. Such "mathematical-mechanical capriccios"[58] bore witness both to the indisputable materiality of even the most immaterial-seeming forces and the importance of pleasure, not pain, in intellectual training. *Delectare et doce* would become the hallmark of the philosophical "recreations" encouraged by the Order.[59]

Cabinets of curiosities, composed of various woods with marble, ivory, snakeskin, enamel, or tortoiseshell inlays, simultaneously revealed and concealed the discontinuities that went into forming them. Collecting was synonymous with patterning. Not unlike the cosmos, artificial worlds required an individual hand to order them and an embodied eye to perceive

65. Unknown, *Display Cabinet,* 1620–1630.

them. Disparate objects, gathered in different places and at separate times, had to be "hyperlinked" through the viewer's insightful "jumps." Simultaneously homogeneous and heterogeneous, the knowledge produced in this network of intersecting coordinates was synthetic.[60] To think in the presence of a cryptic *Wunderkammer,* like the algebraic generation of new concepts in Leibniz's epistemology, required a calculus of combinations for inferring the connections among thousands of unknown aspects or ci-

66. Lucas Cranach, *Reliquary Containing Flayed Skin of Face of St. Bartholomew,* 1519.

Zcum eilfften/Ein sil=
bern monstrenzlein mit.iij.
glesern/Doz Jnne ist/ Vom
finger Zacharie/doran noch
harot.ij.partickel.Ein stuck
vom finger des heilige sant
Hieronymi mit der harot/
ij.partickel.Ein stuck vom
finger sant Georgen /auch
mit der harot.

K ij

Süma.vi.partickel

67. Lucas Cranach (?), *Silver Monstrance with
Three Glass Vials Containing the Fingers of
Zacharias, St. Hieronymus, and a Fragment of
the Finger of St. George,* 1519.

phers.[61] Leibniz hoped that this *mathesis universalis,* or system of universal knowledge, would lead to a transdisciplinary "art of conjecture" (*ars conjectandi*) helping us to arrive at legitimate hypotheses about an increasingly complex universe. His vision was of a hyperworld: less a multitude of particular persons and more a system of relations in which any person might be put together with any circumstance. This jump to establish parallels between symbols, marks, characters, people, and cases dangerously transgressed disciplinary boundaries and organic and inorganic hierarchies. Combinatorics, by definition, valorized intermediary relations, profoundly challenging Descartes's divorce between objective and subjective knowledge.[62] Like plastic Lego blocks,[63] a few kinds of elements were used to construct an infinite variety of different, coexisting objects whose meaning depended on how they became integrated into other activities.

An encyclopedist and a utopian social designer, Leibniz pictured the cosmos not as it appeared when reflected, static and flat, within a conventional looking glass. Instead, he posited a magically illusionistic realm of repeatable objects, beheld from various perspectives. These apparitions seemed animated as they projected their three-dimensionalized shape outward from the bulging convexities of a bewitching sorcière mirror toward a particular viewer (fig. 68). In this ontologized theory of perception, the substance of every living thing acted as the unique point of view of its soul.[64] The body, then, behaved as if it were wearing a pair of multifaceted spectacles through which the soul apprehended its environment in a slivered and distinctively personal way (fig. 69). Each distinct locus of matter looked out from its own angled vantage and re-presented to itself the aspect it witnessed. Obviously influenced by the seventeenth-century development of the life-size camera obscura, Leibniz's windowless global mechanics—like the single-aperture optical tent it mimicked—was immersive. Its purpose was to disappear in the act of apprehension.

The doctrine of preestablished harmony is the ultimate logic of the link. Like a digital computer, the system is both automatic and interactive. Monads are caught up endlessly in feedback loops. Because of their divinely synchronized relation to other monads, perception comes in waves rippling across an immense reflecting pool "through the continual fulgurations of the Divinity, from moment to moment, limited by the receptivity of the creature, to whom limitation is essential."[65] In this manner God transmits the contents of our consciousness directly, vertically to all minds,

68. Anonymous, *Sorcière Mirror,* 18th century.

and they reimage, repurpose, or rearrange information horizontally among themselves. For Leibniz, then, the world is an infinity of converging series, capable of being extended into each other around unique points. Significantly, a sophisticated theory of analogy drives the entire system: "Now this connection, or this adaptation of all created things to each and of each to all, brings it about that each simple substance has relations which express all the others, and that, consequently, it is a perpetual living mirror of the universe."[66]

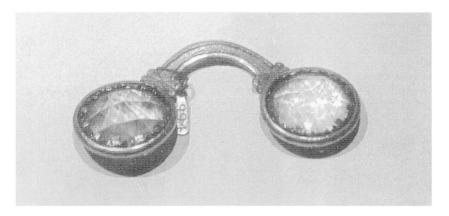

69. Anonymous, *Multiplying Spectacles,* c. 1650.

He illustrates this scheme of obtaining as great a variety as possible while maintaining the greatest possible order by alluding to one of those "digital" cabinets or catoptrical theaters constructed by the Jesuits (fig. 70). Faceted walls, floors, wings multiplied and modified enshrined tiny bits of cork, vegetation, coins, medals, stones, miniature figures, and diminutive buildings to infinity.

And as the same city looked at from different sides appears entirely different, and is as if multiplied perspectively; so also it happens that, as a result of the infinite multitude of simple substances, there are as it were so many different universes, which are nevertheless only the perspectives of a single one, according to the different points of view of each monad.[67]

Like the concept of "schema" in twentieth-century logic, each universe operates like a sort of chunking matrix,[68] that is, a device for structuring a complex situation or set of inputs into an organized whole. Leibniz is also not far afield from the schema theory of Gestalt psychology, attempting to relate universals to particulars in accessible ways. Our individual cases, like our discrete perceptions, are always part of a collective experience. They remain exemplary while interconnected within larger, dynamic structures.

Although all monads experience the same world in its totality, they

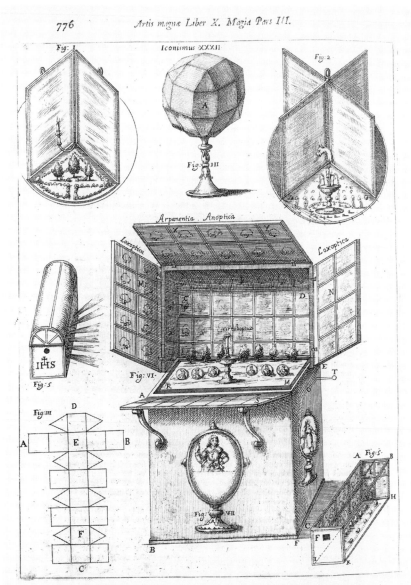

70. Athanasius Kircher, *Glazed Cabinet,* 1671.

only clearly experience their part of the world.[69] Prophetic of Seurat's divisionist method, all phenomena—whether large or small—must be reduced to irradiated dots to establish the preestablished harmony of the soul and the body, the equilibrium of the one and the many. For, at every moment, numberless noisy perceptions exist within us—like the distant roar of the ocean—but without rising to consciousness through the focusing of apperception and reflection.

These *minute (petites) perceptions* are then of greater influence because of their consequences than is thought. It is they which form I know not what, these tastes, these images of the sensible qualities, clear in the mass but confused in the parts, these impressions which surrounding bodies make upon us, which embrace the infinite, this connection which each being has with all the rest of the universe. It may even be said that in consequence of these minute perceptions the present is big with the future and laden with the past, that all things conspire . . . and that in the least of substances eyes as piercing as those of God could read the whole course of the things in the universe.[70]

Both microscopic and telescopic, Leibniz's philosophy is intrinsic to the baroque habit of seeing double. Acrobatically balancing incongruities in a "convergent contrapposto,"[71] he married narrow sharpness to a widening perspective. Like Bill Viola's contemplative video installation, *Room for St. John of the Cross* (1983), the still, small spark of the self is coordinated with a vast and tumultuous panorama ceaselessly unfurling outside it (fig. 71). The analogical universe emerged in the *Monadology* as simultaneously protean and fixed, regulated and mutable, sublimely theatrical and unnaturally fake.

Leibniz's metaphysics also constituted the only major modern system that situated analogy within an ontology that was, at the same time, an aesthetics. With the exception of Deleuze, current philosophers have consistently ignored or underrated Leibniz's aesthetics, while Kant's, to my mind, has been overrated precisely because it was allegorical.[72] From the treatise *Towards a Universal Characteristic* (1677), to the *Principles of a Logical Calculus* (c. 1679), to the monumental response to Locke, the *New Essays on the Human Understanding* (1704), through the *Monadology* and the final *Theodicy* (1710), Leibniz's kaleidoscopic world view was deeply visual and analogical. Perfection, for him, meant that diversity had been molded into

71. Bill Viola, *Room for St. John of the Cross,*
1983.

perceptible unity and coherence.[73] Nevertheless, he insisted that each monad was different from every other. "For there are never in nature two
beings which are exactly alike and in which it is not possible to find an
internal difference, or one founded upon an intrinsic quality."[74]

This thesis appears to be vindicated in advanced scientific studies of
what might be called visual ecology. Studies of opsin, a molecule that can
snap into a different shape in trillionths of a second when exposed to light,
is offering clues to the evolution of vision. In the eye, opsin absorbs pho-
tons and initiates a cascade of biochemical events that coalesce as an image
in the brain. Various versions of the molecule allow different organisms
to see color differently. In learning the structure of the genes for opsins,
scientists are beginning to understand why some people are much more
sensitive to red, or why primates have evolved a color vision that is trichro-
matic, based on red, green, and blue, unlike the yellow-blue system of most
mammals.[75] What is positively Leibnizian about this research is that it
proves that the smallest possible genetic difference between two human

beings makes a large perceptual difference in how they apprehend the world. The problem remaining is to demonstrate the mechanisms of confluence, how contrasts produce harmony.

It is not accidental, as romantic color theorist George Field remarked, that chromatics was the ultimate instantiation of a *"Universal Archetype."*[76] "For all analogy is founded on *universal relations,* or the universe would not be a system of order and wisdom, but a chaos of confusion and folly, without unity, harmony, or design."[77] Trinitarian coincidence in optics harked back to the Newtonian generation of a "union" of primaries in a prism. These separate hues were first broken and then joined in concord. The formerly discordant three became "one without distinction."[78] Thus the concurrence of chromatic variety, like Leibniz's *Monadology,* resembled "the *universe of which it is a part"*; it was "an *absolute unity,* comprehending a *relative infinity—a PERFECT SYSTEM!"*[79]

The skeletal automata ornamenting sixteenth- and seventeenth-century clocks struck the death of the hour. Their hammering signaled the end of a sequence of unduplicatable moments. Yet no day is brand new. Remember Hume's unmasking of humanity's constant conjunction of rising with setting sun[80] and Nietzsche's lament over the everlasting return of everything that went before.[81] Living in a society means learning, largely automatically, to repeat forms of behavior that already exist. But this replication of the past, as Valerio Valeri emphasized concerning the ties between genealogy and Hawaiian kingship mythology, does not preclude innovation. A remote period in which one is always able to discover some precedent for some current action, no matter how new, can hardly be accused of being static or of merely reproducing itself stereotypically. As this anthropologist of the South Pacific region observed: "All cultures with a historical tradition have maintained that the past offers a repertory of rules, of connections among types of actions and types of consequences, in the form of concrete events that can be analogically related to the present."[82] Precisely because this correlation between what has been and what is or will be is *analogical* (i.e., based on recognizing similarities as much as differences), it does not replicate hallowed models but enables their comparison.

Jeff Wall's backlit Cibachrome transparency *A Sudden Gust of Wind (after Hokusai)* visualizes such complex layerings of singularity and collectivity and so restores to view the connections between ongoing history and the contingent present (fig. 72).[83] His lambent work exemplifies the opera-

72. Jeff Wall, *A Sudden Gust of Wind (after Hokusai),* 1993.

tions of the analogical imagination,[84] in which the reflective mind searches for some order while recognizing that, at every instant, it needs some similarities-in-difference, some analogues, some past systems of order in the face of chance. The frozen figures, assuming poses subtly borrowed from a famous nineteenth-century Japanese woodblock print, stand scattered across a fluorescent, windswept landscape to coalesce in a decisive snapshot. Each person in the scene responds separately to the intrusion of accident. Nature and art are thus components in an endless creative dialectic, part of the repeated, yet novel, ambivalences between a second of time and the slow flow of duration.

A persistent dialogue between sameness and difference, originality and mimicry, is a constant feature of Wall's work. *The Ventriloquist at a Birthday Party in October 1947* (1990), for example, plays up the uniqueness and repeatability characteristic of any performance. But the fact that this magic show has as its centerpiece a wooden doll—resembling a boy dressed in a fancy historical costume—and that this dummy becomes enlivened through the projection of a woman's voice imitating that of a man, complicates the nexus of relationships. Moreover, the contrived "realism" of the entranced audience composed of children obviously belonging to another era, yet captured in a recent photograph, dovetails with Wall's subtle evocation of artificial life forms. Old-fashioned puppet, after all, exists on the same developmental trajectory as automaton and robot.

The bobbing balloons, preternaturally frozen in midair, confirm by their ironic stability the disjunction between past and present. To be sure, the scene is commemorated, the artifact remains; it is the anonymous procession of museum onlookers who surge forward. Integrating two fundamental types of "photography as art"—the photojournalistic model and the cinematic model[85]—Wall produces novel combinations. He forces the relationship between these two opposites by juxtaposing the camera shutter's ability to register the image instantaneously and our awareness of the implied presence of the photographic apparatus in the process of picture-making. This facility in connecting the seemingly unconnected enables him to link the temporal nature of photography to its inherent spatiality.

Analogy—whether in myth, philosophy, religion, history, or aesthetics—grappled with the problem of how to conjoin an accumulated body of practices to the shifting present and elusive future. Within this developmental, not revolutionary, framework, the birth of the new was always apparitional, the astonishing product of an artful combination of preexisting elements. This generative potency, as we saw, was conceived basically in sexual and magical terms. Transformation always arose at the intersection of constancy with instability, coupling continuity to discontinuity.

As Francis Bacon insisted in the *Novum Organum* (1620), alterations in nature take place by degrees, by means of small transitions (*per minima*) as difficult to perceive as the molecules out of which they are composed. This doctrine of hidden order and of matter's individual particulars as transformations into new forms of what was given in another form continuously binds together different moments of organic development.[86] Nature's process of induction resembles the method of one of its tiny creatures, the bee, which assimilates and changes what it collects by working it up into its own substance. Singular instances, during the abstracting process of being intercompared with other cases, become raised into real resemblances, abridged concentrations that are more intellectually robust than merely solitary phenomena. Although he is considered a founder of modern empirical science, Bacon's theory of continuity—passing through many middle terms or gradations—is indebted to the analogical thought of Plato and the Neoplatonists which he systematized into a coordinating challenge directed at natural philosophy. How do you tie the extraordinary together with the ordinary; how do you situate the heteroclite object within a more general recurring order?

For media-saturated postmodernists, nothing gives a better sense of the ancient thaumaturgical process of cosmic transmutation than an entrancing Siegfried and Roy spectacle at the Mirage. In one set of their Las Vegas extravaganza, Siegfried transforms a voluptuous Valkyrie into Roy, then transforms Roy into an eagle, and then himself into Roy.[87] Sudden changes of gender, historical epoch, character, genre are an apparently effortless succession of illusions, a stream of analogies, virtuoso technical effects, and rococo atmospheric tableaux overlaid onto the eternal colorless and tasteless atoms that make up humdrum ordinary reality. This Ovidian wizardry, no less than Jupiter's easy assumption of animal disguises, establishes an instantaneous rapport with the audience. And why not? We are all enchanted by incantatory scenes of resurrection and reconciliation. We all long for the disappearance of what we hate and the reappearance of those we love.

4

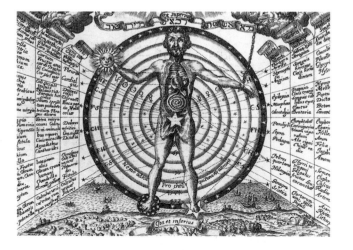

Recombinancy: Binding the Computational "New Mind" to the Combinatorial "Old Mind"

There is one fact about the brain so obvious it's seldom mentioned: it's attached to the rest of the body and communicates with it.
Sir Francis Crick, The Astonishing Hypothesis

Our analogical adventure begins and ends in the present. If the pre-Cartesians divined more in intelligence than desire-free calculation, the contemporary world also seems alive to the mobility and cross-prompting of human thought. Nowhere is the tension more in evidence between virtual devices bound to algorithmic processes and the nonformalizable moments of flexible insight than in the scientific debates swirling around the nature of consciousness. In light of these difficulties, this chapter considers two intertwined topics. First, it puts an intrinsically visual analogy to work on a pair of major questions now preoccupying the philosophy of mind. These are the binding problem and the nature of qualia. Second, it claims that neuroscientists need to consider the complex ways in which art shapes the perpetual flux of sensory information to fully understand the operations of the visual brain.

Along the way, I argue that we realize something constructive when we see. We do not merely illustrate or copy what is given, but give birth to something that would not otherwise exist. Seeing is about being struck that something is, or can be, connected to something else. The visual arts, as especially high-order forms of envisioning, make an elusive personal awareness substantially real in an external realization. They help us understand the myriad modes by which people endlessly modify and reuse the elements available to them. They thus provide new data about the concurrence of sensory experience and the indivisibility of brain and body that could augment cognitive science.

I support this claim through the examination of interwoven styles that conspicuously expose their seamed manufacture. Cabinets of curiosities, Piranesi etchings, cubist collages, dada-inspired boxes, even the Netscape browser or Macintosh's mosaic toolbar—all provide information about some connective aspects of cognition that are not well captured by the scientific approaches currently adopted. Second, I propose that this analogical thinking about thinking yields a more complex psychological picture of the decentered self. That artful machine, the reciprocal desktop computer, challenges both Kant's view of the transcendental subject as the unifying locus of experience and deconstructionism's romantic dissolution of identity into the twin negatives of indeterminacy and undecidability.

Perhaps one of the most intriguing items for the new study of consciousness to consider is what, so far, has not been considered. Why is this exploding area of research, intent on discovering the relation of the brain to human awareness, not multidisciplinary enough? Why does it look primarily to text-based fields, rather than the imaging arts, for insight on how cognition actually works?[1] Let me put the question positively. What light might a humanities-based imagist shed on the binding problem perplexing analytical philosophers, cognitive scientists, computer programmers, neurophysiologists or neuroanatomists, linguists, and both "strong" and "weak" AI proponents?

While there has been a recent surge of interest in the "prehistory of the mind" and the "archaeology of cognition,"[2] rhetoric's combinatorics and the aesthetics of the perceptual jump have not been considered in the search to explain how discrete mental functions work in concert. Even Jerome Bruner's distinction between a logical computationalism and a technical-social culturism does not adequately take into account the ways in which mental activity is visually, not just narratively, situated.[3]

We lack a deeper, richer understanding of the nonverbal "inner life" of the self.[4] I propose, then, that it would prove illuminating for a non-neurobiological field—particularly one with a visual and historical focus—to address the puzzle of the mind from a perspective other than the coded logic of "thinking machines" and reverse engineering. As the French installation artist Christian Boltanski declared: "Each of us is a unit filled with small memories."[5]

The challenge to produce a coordinated understanding of psychological and mental efforts calls for a new discipline, one that ties together the complex biology of the mammalian visual system with a humanistically grounded theory of perception. The term "Neuronal Aesthetics," coined by Olaf Breidbach and Karl Clausberg,[6] captures the fact that we are not only figuratively, but increasingly actually, enveloped inside and out by technologically generated images.[7] This emergent field would have neurobiologists and historians of every facet of conception working together. I see my contribution to the formulation of such a futuristic interdisciplinary venture as demonstrating the unifyingly visual aspects of mentalese, the inseparability of form and content in analogical combinatorics.

I say this while realizing the still mysterious operations of internal representation. What to do in an era when the Lockean view of the mind as a wax tablet receiving impressions from the ambient is untenable? Yet, paradoxically, this outer world is available to us only through sensory streams which, with the help of cell assemblies inside the head, become indirectly aggregated into concepts and notions that we represent to ourselves. One sees the world, then, only as one can. We now know that the brain is not instructed by specific objects; instead, the environment becomes reconfigured when somato-optically projected onto the cerebral cortex. Sensory cells, therefore, do not merely copy the external physical reality to which they correspond. Rather, they react to a specific stimulus by slightly altering its physiological constitution. In a light-sensitive cell, for example, the capture of a photon initiates a complex cascade of chemical reactions that alters the membrane of the receptor cell.[8]

But this capture is itself dependent upon an organism's particular situation, since neural networks (or a general-purpose learning "machinery" forming the basis for all human cognition) are the result of individual developments, the ontogenies of specific organisms. Such symbiotic construction can be stated in terms of evolutionary theory: organisms actively shape their environments by correlating an exterior to an interior architecture over time. That inside and outside "fit" is the result of a selective evolution that weeds out those things that do not mesh with an individual neuronal landscape.

Importantly, then, there is a *history* to natural selection, and these historical causes lead, via the genes, to constraints on processes and structures operating here and now.[9] While the invariant underlying structure of nerve cells appears very early in a species, later baroque variations emerge not only by chance but as a result of working over existing materials. Epigenesis captures this notion that individual development is not a simple unfolding of some innate potential but a highly variable activity resulting from immensely complicated interactions between genetic information, the developing features of an organism or group, and the mutable environment. Precisely because of this historical dimension, the varied instantiations of culture, too, represent such a group-level phenomenon. More to the point, the visual arts, as an important subset of the latter, have produced concrete images exhibiting how the visual system in the brain individually maps the changing internal and external scene. This complex constructing, going on over long stretches of time, not only responds to shifts in the lifeworld but helps shape adaptive learning. Discrete and collective selections made in the past become gradually or suddenly imprinted on a specific social milieu.

But to revert to the inner scenery: recent experiments with insects, cats, and monkeys have shown the stunning connectivity characterizing neural nets. Individual nerve cells are tied not just to their neighbors. Clusters of neurons, in fact, are in direct contact with a patchwork of defined nerve cells located both in their own and in the opposite hemisphere.[10] The dynamics of these oscillating or rippling coactivation processes have, so far, eluded the cybernetic model of information as a constant alternation between binary oppositions (stimulus and response, input and output) used in computer simulations. Nor have the neurosciences, to date, been able to explain the collaging of thought processes neuronally.

My point is that the fireworks set off across the brain when it is excited by a single stimulus oblige us to consider that organ as a variously textured unity. These activity bursts, erupting both in surrounding and distant areas of the matrix, produce a tapestry of interwoven patterns, not the mechanical "nesting"[11] of differentiated activities discussed in the robotics literature. Given this high-level associative architecture, what is the nature of the correspondences linking discrete, distributed neurons whose firings are not isomorphic with the appearance of an external object but analogous to the combined look and feel of it?

Parallel distributed systems certainly describe some characteristics of real biological networks, especially the representation of sensorial information by a discrete set of neurons.[12] Information theory and information processing, however, are not compelling when it comes to explaining the evaluation that occurs of such an input. Computers remain mute about the sophisticated interplay between intuition, will, discrimination, memory, and knowledge formation in humans. An adequate description of this holistic aspect of sentience—by which complicated ideas spring from the syntactic combination of simpler ones and are judged[13]—has eluded researchers who view the brain as a mechanism for less-than-speedy calculation or as a purely computational infrastructure.

How we couple representations in space is the key to understanding selfhood. The activity of linking has an emotional component, fitting our desires to an expanding universe of events in which both self and others are mutually transformed. We need, then, to recorporealize not only the visual but the mental order. Human intelligence exhibits itself in artistic inter- and intrasubjective powers for bringing worlds together. It displays itself externally in mirroring moments of extension (fig. 73). Single vision becomes multiplied, shattered, and reconfigured as it is dynamically relayed within an infinite network of compossible perceptions.

While life is continuously making itself present to us, it is seldom present to us as we would wish.[14] Images set before us untranslatable and irreducible patterns—from the traditional spectrum of multicolored graphics, to flickering videos, to the latest scintillating icons on screen. These variously record the nuanced perceptual adjustments of our ongoing accommodation to people, places, and things. This human conjunctive faculty is simultaneously individual and global, specific and general, capable of engendering figures of differentiation and reconciliation.

Analogy's comparative drive to map across knowledge systems is also helpful in conceptualizing the myriad ways in which the psyche suffers dislocations requiring the reintegration of disconnected components into a whole. Feeling the aggressive pull of a doubled, split, or multiple personality competing for attention—in the past and present—has prompted medical efforts to reassociate the mind's dissociated segments into a single self.[15] While an analogical inquiry into the attempts to heal such fragmenting psychological conditions would be useful, I want to focus, instead, on two contemporary biological riddles.

The intractable problem of synthesis lies at the heart of both. Francis Crick declared that solving the first conundrum was central to providing a systematic account of higher-order consciousness. Among notable neuroscientists to accord vision the cognitive seriousness it deserves, Crick spoke of the enigma of how various stimuli to different portions of the brain become married, as if by enchantment, to produce a single experience of an object within an existential subject.[16] How can a unified image emerge from the four parallel systems working in the visual cortex? These must be linked at every level into a vast network of reentrant connections allowing information to flow back and forth in synchrony so that perception and comprehension occur simultaneously.[17]

The second puzzle emerges from the pictorial nature of consciousness, the fact that we have a vivid internal picture of the external world. Yet the

73. Lucas Samaras, *Mirrored Room*, 1966.

difficulty of conveying these intensely and personally experienced qualia to others with verbal or numerical precision (i.e., the redness of red, the painfulness of pain) makes it impossible to assess their exact role in consciousness or to find neural correlates for them.[18] Owen Flanagan wonderfully termed this distinctive and elusive subjectivity, which each of us feels is "like" us, the "missing shade of you."[19] The mystery is how we see things as shared; how different parts of the brain learn to harmonize. By what means do the diverse perceptions gathered by our five senses become assimilated within the brain and then sedimented into an intimately private, yet simultaneously cultural and social, identity?

By recuperating the sophisticated workings of ancient analogy for modern science, I believe artists and art, architecture, design, film, and media historians, in particular, can contribute a cross-cortical model of the complex processes of mental combination. Types of images that conspicuously do not blend their elements are especially effective in demonstrating the rules governing the brain's connectivity, how it is able to activate many discrete areas possessing specific functions and juxtapose them into a larger coherent pattern. Perceptually combined information not only avoids the intellectual limitations of linearity but reveals our constant involvement in heterogeneous reasoning.[20] Images that show this weaving of two or more forms of representation provide information about the complexity of cooperation that has eluded exclusively scientific or computational investigations.

We will look at some important artistic genres, past and present, that conspicuously cross-thread modalities. They reveal how viewers create analogies in response to the interactive pressures exerted by a noncoalescent work of art. When confronting an apparently "chaotic" tangle, individuals, irrespective of their social and cultural differences, must quilt these simultaneously occurring variegated stimuli together into a personal interpretation. The external patterns assumed by this subjective process mimic the brain's internal piecing together of a diversified input. We know that the brain's stored visual memory system for objects is based on many cells, each one responsive to one view alone, integrating lines, angles, and directions over time into an ensemble that permits an entire cell cluster to recognize something as a particular entity.[21] Because it is not preblended, braiding collage obliges us to see ourselves mentally laboring to combine many shifting and conflicting perceptions into a unified representation.

While it is true that the interpretation of a work of art will change over time and place as social, cultural, and intellectual traditions change, the fact remains that there seems to be a general ongoing struggle to fit one's evolving conceptual system to the unstable elements of a wider environment. Such wrestling does not appear to be optional for human beings. Stitched-together styles thus hold a special interest for neuroscientists because they expose the jolting ways one's concepts intersect with an ambient already prestocked with "natural" items and ready-made artifacts.

Although we can no longer speak, in the empiricist sense, of having a picture of the outside world, the observer still needs to "image" the specific relationship obtaining between the liquidity of her personal awareness and an obdurate reality. If part of what it takes for an object to be considered real is its resistance to us, then its particularity is definable as "a located patch of metaphysical flux."[22] Laced-together genres oblige the viewer to stumble over such momentary solidifications occurring in the visual field and so to individuate them. Paradoxically, such blockings underscore the stony specificities of our own self. Yet the fragility of objective and subjective coherence also makes us conscious of how contingent, jumbled, and nonlapidary all material things, including ourselves, in fact are.

The cubist portrait/still lifes of Braque, Gris, and Picasso, as Pierre Reverdy remarked, show how subjectivity exists in interaction with an environment characterized by spatial flux, not rigid geometries.[23] The enfolding of an inner self, the four walls of a room, and the outside world demonstrates the French poet's conviction that consciousness comes into being just as objects come into being: because of their relations. This sentiment comes remarkably close to a central idea in recent, counter-inert and non-hard-edged AI, namely that the processes of producing mental representations and manipulating them are inextricably intertwined.[24] The difference is that these machine models, unlike works of art, are highly abstract and simplified.

We also become aware of awareness only in the drive to connect. Attention is labor-intensive. Charles Saunders Peirce, in trying to overcome "Secondness," the primal condition in which consciousness found itself in confrontation with things and at a distance from other minds, had the Real forcing its way to recognition as something other than the mind's creation. Only through reaction, visual complication, conflict was "Thirdness" achieved, that pragmatic relatedness to other phases of experience.[25]

Peirce's phenomenology underscored the importance of analogy, since this helped to articulate features of reality in a way that accommodated the pervasive textures, "traits," and "tones or tints" to which we are individually attuned.[26]

For Peirce, as for Leibniz, knowing is perspectival. Similarly, by denying the conventional distinction between thought and action, John Dewey argued that comprehension consisted not in seizing something accurately from the outside, but in practically and experimentally engaging in events in a purposive, intelligent way.[27] In either case, reality is the end product of the imaginative creation of categories we constantly stretch out to grasp.

Whether participating in a common outer life or making sense of the varieties of inner experience, understanding occurs as the consequence of an expenditure of psychic and physical energy compelling disparate things to converge. The in-betweenness of assemblage—those body-object amalgams composed of tossed scraps, found objects, organic and inorganic remnants—embodies this stunning spectrum of relocatable patterns available to human subjectivity. Collage, as the process of transforming ephemera by cutting and pasting them into momentarily stable configurations, continues to be a particularly effective technique for capturing the chimera of consciousness in action. We literally see how the brain organizes incoming visual stimuli by witnessing how perceptual organization begins by distinguishing salient features, to recombine bits and pieces and process them unequally in the mind's eye.[28]

Originating with the cubists and expanded by the dadaists and surrealists, this "gluing" of transitory detritus has extended into montage, film editing, and now computer manipulation and body art (fig. 74). Severing and then recompounding incongruous parts—like Nina Levy's witty sculpture of a candy-pink tongue licking a fleshy hand—reconceptualized male and female sexual relations as the fleeting contact between temporarily exaggerated, far-fetched elements. Such startling conjunctions tend to break duality-establishing boundaries, whether in art or in science.[29]

Like the cross-kingdom biological fusions currently being fabricated by University of California at Berkeley scientist David Ow—who welded together the genetic substance of a firefly and tobacco to form phosphorescent plants—photomontage artists in the past merged, substituted, and mutated aspects of one species of imagery with those of another. In the futuristic comparatist series *From an Ethnographic Museum* (1925), the Ber-

74. Nina Levy, *Hobby,* 1995.

lin dadaist Hannah Höch produced precarious fusions of anthropological artifacts with human forms. These fetishes for a new eugenics—redolent of familiar and unfamiliar objects—radiate an odd beauty. The face of a black or West Indian woman wears the disconcerting graft of a rosebud mouth. Tatters of a white face are interspersed with those of a chimpanzee, resulting in startling mixed-race idols.[30]

Robert Rauschenberg's hybrid "combines" from the 1950s and 1960s exploited collage materials to knit together far-flung associations. A dizzying host of autobiographical and personal references are interwoven with intersecting sets of overlapping images.[31] Fragments engage in a suggestive dialogue across the vast surfaces of these multidirectional and nonhierarchical paintings, whose meaning is impossible to pin down with precision. Literally hundreds of photographs, familiar pieces of packaging, flour sacks, wrecked machinery, silk screens, and solvent transfers of *Scientific American* illustrations are stage-managed into an interlocking order.[32] The artist sifted and recombined the unsorted pile of offerings proffered by the visual world in which we actually live and work, in a feat of selection still remarkable in our computer era.

Beverly Fishman, using laser color copiers and overpainted photographic images that are thickly resin-coated to suggest the surface of a lens, instantiates genetic replication by duplicating it in her own artistic procedures (fig. 75). Collaging and altering images culled from technical texts, she develops analogies to cellular structures through the doubling of sleek elliptical shapes or the spherical whirling of biological matter and star clusters. The body's tiny galaxies as well as immense nebulae become coordinates in a vast, interrelated system (fig. 76). Microscopic fragments mimic telescopic constellations when viewed from inside the primal cosmic soup.

The increasing "techno-seduction"[33] of artists not only provides them with new content and innovative forms of presentation, but allots them a constitutive role in making difficult-to-imagine constructs comprehensible. Suzanne Anker, in her installation piece *Zoosemiotics*, set a large glass globe filled with water in the center of a gallery. Silvery sculptural simulations of animal chromosomes, distributed in random, mostly circular order across the room's four walls, were magnified within it (fig. 77). Gazelle, frog, fish, and primate (gorilla, chimpanzee, orangutan, gibbon) genetic material became dramatically compressed within the mirroring walls of this transparent vessel. Coalescence had the additional effect of metamor-

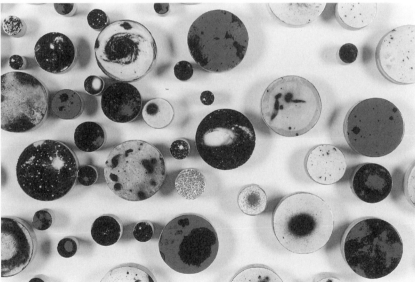

75. Beverly Fishman, *A.x. #1-96,* 1996.

76. Beverly Fishman, *A.x. #1-96,* detail.

77. Suzanne Anker, *Zoosemiotics,* 1995.

phosing the disparate X-shapes into miniature bodies dancing on the curved sides of the container and swimming within the transparent liquid. Consequently, the beaker acted as a powerful reflecting lens, changing the appearance of the contents depending on the position of the viewer. This optical abstraction, anthropomorphizing, and transformation of linguistic grids and codes into cavorting figures offers a striking parallel to the selective fashioning of graffiti-like experience into a coherent self by the mind.

Similarly, in Orshi Drozdik's process piece *Erythrocytes* (1988), the stationing of a convex lens mounted on a rod and sited in front of a sea of sculptured cells invited individual beholders to focalize, personalize, and internalize an anonymous body's microphenomena. This non-Cartesian way of seeing illuminates how alien things, in order to be felt and understood, must become incorporated into our very substance. As in Epicurean optics, we look at the world and it looks back. I am suggesting, then, that the brain's "binding" capacity, no less than gene splicing or blood chemistry, can be externalized for scrutiny precisely in those aesthetic situations when it yokes variegated experiences and makes them proximate for a specific viewer.

Crick's formulation of the "binding problem" restates the great epistemological riddle of abstraction. Here we need to venture into a short explanatory excursus. In the second chapter of *Body Criticism*, I argued that there were two major strands of cognitive compression running through Western thought. Taken together, these complementary activities image two different properties of brain function: the conscious, analytical decomposition of information and the unconscious, holistic intuition of a topic in its entirety preceding awareness. These forms of selective epitomization also correspond to dual philosophical methods: deduction as quantitative determination and induction as the empirical collection of innumerable cases needing to be surveyed.

These opposed procedures for distilling or collating materials possess a distinctive look and come dressed in specific aesthetic styles. The first calls up a purist, so-to-speak Miesian "modernist" minimalism that has the mind dissecting flesh from idea to arrive at a geometric Absolute. The second invokes a prismatic, Frank Gehryan, if you will, "postmodernist" syncretism that has the mind stitching chaotic appearances together, placing novel findings in contact with existing knowledge so that the old becomes simultaneously constructed and deconstructed by the new. Certain types

78. Anonymous, *Crank Magic Lantern Slide with Kaleidoscopic Design,* 19th century.

of art are especially successful in exhibiting the interplay between such symbolic and subsymbolic mental operations.

Additionally, it may help to imagine such mental sorting and correlating of contrary visual information as akin to Henry James's refraction of marred individuals through the translucent sides of a golden bowl. That beautiful, but subtly cracked, crystal goblet served the novelist as a kaleidoscope for revealing the singularly flawed temperaments of his personae, their healthy or unhealthy consciousness (fig. 78). When given a twist and held up to the light, the lenslike fissure in a gilded glass became visible, suggesting an analogy to the splintering of brittle inner being. A chromatically complex mosaic arose only when specific pressure was applied to the structurally weakest point of a character.

In a powerful synthesis—now realizable because of the development of video technology—James anticipated Bill Viola's reflection, in *Heaven and Earth* (1992), of one unique face in that of an antithetical other, resulting from the interaction of two screens. Startling dualities are always on the verge of coalescence but never, finally, cohere. This Janus-face of abstraction—as both quintessence and chromatics, directional spotlight and convulsive flicker—captures the brain's preferential mechanism in action. Paring permits it to eliminate some neuronal groups while strengthening others, while pairing opens up new possibilities allowing us to generalize and learn over time.

Box art in the twentieth century (spanning from Marcel Duchamp's *Boîte-en-valise* to Lucas Samaras's glass, fur, or needle-lined coffers and compartments) represents an intensification of collage practices (see fig. 73). It, too, divides physical existence into the hard-edged container and the always-escaping stream of the contained.[34] If, for the Duchamp of the hermetic *Large Glass* (1915–1923), "the conjunction of the two things [words and images] entirely removes the retinal aspect I don't like,"[35] his bird cage playfully filled with *trompe-l'oeil* marble sugar cubes tells another story. *Why Not Sneeze Rrose Sélavy?* (1921) taunts the cubists for their literal use of blocks and grids, mimetically punning Picasso's and Braque's analytical pictorial elements. Yet this witty container is something more than a nasty joke directed at the intellectual pretensions of an art movement Duchamp despised.[36] Its blatant disruption of optical and tactile experiences reveals how the mind jumps to new concepts when forced to yoke the contradictory information arising from each of the five senses. In essence a three-dimensional rebus,[37] the Duchampian readymade sparks the leap to coordinate detached or divided associations.

Resembling the chambered brain in its ability to store, conserve, memorialize, but above all assemble and transmute an amazing, even paradoxical, variety of things within its confines, the mnemonic box throughout history was the epitome of a malleable universe finely adjusted to the conflicting emotions of its owner (fig. 79). Its ancestor was the memory palace of the Roman orators. Ideas, recollections, persons, and feelings were draped around rooms or placed on furnishings and then were verbally "picked up" by rhetors, such as Cicero and Quintilian, in the order in which they were to be discussed.[38] It was thus possible to ally thoughts and events with specific forms and shapes in a mentalized architecture of places. In the 1530s Giulio Camillo designed an actual "theater" in which half the audience could stand up on a central stage to gaze upon the images arranged in the stands.[39] And we know that, in 1596, the Jesuit Matteo Ricci taught the Chinese to erect an ambitious but fictive pavilion filled

79. Anonymous, *Toy (Boxed) Globe Showing Captain Cook's Voyages,* c. 1840–1860.

with evocative figures for the mental traveler to collect on his conceptual voyage.[40]

The densely associative vitrine constructions of Joseph Cornell, in more recent times, captured the roamable spaces of human consciousness: ever present and ever in the past. Significantly, Cornell referred to himself as a "designer," not an artist, and saw himself as a magician in the tradition of the *supernaturaliste* Gérard de Nerval, and the symbolist *magus* extolled by Mallarmé.[41] He never thought of his shadow boxes as "mere" sculpture, but as static theater, poetic enactments, surrealist scenarios. These "toys for mathematicians," enshrining different levels of rebuslike imagery, precipitated mental journeys flowing backward and forward in time and across space. Deeply personal to the artist, these haunting environments caging the visible also touch museum goers by provoking a flow of explicit and implicit memories.[42] Suggestive objects mobilize our associative faculty and generate bonds between the external and internal world.

In such boxes, indifferent or transitory castoffs—like vanishing sensations—were alchemically metamorphosed into perduring objects for multiple viewers. These perishables preserved, within a sheltering receptacle, did for vision what the *madeleine* did for fragrance. We perceive the transparency of a wine glass, the striations of an agate marble, the gossamer laciness of a Victorian doll, the glow of a sky chart, or the melancholic mauve-washed engraving of a Medici princess, before we *think* them as concepts.

The olfactory epithelium and the limbic system, those oldest parts of the brain from an evolutionary standpoint, remind us that receptor cells fire messages which, in turn, transmit signals flooding us with love, longing, sorrow, joy, and rage. The confounding ways in which scents, savors, sights, and sounds manage, in Kipling's words, to make our "heart-strings crack" raises the other pressing question the new mind researchers, no matter their camp, agree requires resolution. How does the brain produce a cohesive consciousness from physical substances that waft, caress, vacillate, shimmer, or drift outside of us and yet manage to touch and alter us internally? A major and much-disputed factor in the process of cognitive binding is precisely the mysterious role played by qualia.

No one demonstrated better than Joseph Cornell that molding the welter of the passions into manifestly organized compositions is one of the greatest and most difficult achievements of the visual arts. This analogical quest of retrieval, seeking to gather together unattainable presences, is the antithesis of coarse materialism. In a group of boxed "homage-albums" dedicated to nineteenth-century divas such as Fanny Cerrito or Carlotta Grisi, we see how the imaginative depositing of trivia and anecdotes transforms the mundane into mythical experience. This compartmentalization of unattainable desires recalls Emily Dickinson's habit of pinning together and squirreling away her poems—composed on snippets of paper, backs of used envelopes, and overwritten on grocery lists—in a secret drawer or trunk.

In *Taglioni's Jewel Casket*, Cornell, too, collectively housed the adored phantoms of unrequitable longing. This private treasure consists of a blue velvet-lined wooden box that ceremonially offers a crystal necklace elegantly draped above a rising tide of glass cubes. (The version in the Art Institute of Chicago lacks the necklace; fig. 80.) One of a series of *Homages to the Romantic Ballet*, it bears an inscription in Cornell's hand affixed to the inside lid. "On a moonlit night in the winter of 1835 the carriage of Marie Taglioni was halted by a Russian highway man, and that enchanting crea-

80. Joseph Cornell, *Taglioni's Jewel Casket
(Homage to the Romantic Ballet)*, 1942.

ture commanded to dance for this audience of one on a panther's skin spread over the snow beneath the stars. From this actuality arose the legend that to keep alive the memory of this adventure so precious to her, Taglioni formed the habit of placing a piece of artificial ice in her jewel casket or dressing table where, melting among the sparkling stones, there was evoked a hint of the atmosphere of the starlit heavens over the ice-covered landscape."[43]

By giving palpable shape to intensely personal emotions, Cornell unforgettably turned indescribable intimacies into publicly sharable analogies. This age-old search for material equivalences to match the qualitative *feel* of elusive inner states fueled the pursuit of color correspondences (a peculiarly romantic quest engaging various people from Goethe to Delacroix). It continues to drive research into how people are affected by distinctive odors (an old question, underlying the development of the per-

81. Jean-Siméon Chardin, *Still Life with Peaches and Goblet*, c. 1759–1760.

fumer's blending skill as well as early-modern medical therapies directed against airborne contagion). The search for adequate substitutes remains evident in the desire to find visual or verbal parallels for the gamut of tactile pressures the body can undergo (think of Diderot's struggle to inventory Chardin's veiling glazes and textured strokes [fig. 81] or the Marquis de Sade's encyclopedic itemization of erotic palpations). And it lives on when we try to articulate the gustatory pleasures (famously classified by Brillat-Savarin) arising when rolling delicious flavors around the tongue and over the palate. The quest for objective correlatives is thus not about simulation or isomorphism but about experiencing an intense intersection, a crossing-in-the-middle of body and soul before the work.

Historically, such hard-to-systematize sensations posed, and continue to pose, a major difficulty for many scientists and philosophers spanning from Isaac Newton, the British empiricists, up to and including Gerald Edelman. As the Nobel laureate declared in *Bright Air, Brilliant Fire,* we stand at the beginning of the neuroscientific revolution. But the overriding difficulty haunting any scientific attempt to explain the mind is that it arises as a result of physical interactions across an enormously large number of different levels of organization, ranging from the molecular to the social.[44] Presumably, since no two people experience secondary qualities or characteristics (as Shaftesbury notably termed them) exactly alike, how do such variable subjective conditions fit into a *general* theory of consciousness?

This isomorphist quandary—taking similarity to mean exact copy—has led Daniel Dennett, for one, to deny that first-person privilege to conscious states is something relevant for cognitive scientists.[45] To me this seems tantamount to denying the importance of internal mental states altogether, since it reduces them to mere epiphenomena of a material brain. How they occur thus need not be explained. Dennett's neural Darwinianism is a slightly softer version of Paul and Patricia Churchland's robotic model of the brain as computer or information processor, a position that reduces that organ to rapid-fire neuronal operations performed in parallel.[46] Brain scientist Steven Pinker, in *How the Mind Works,* further deconstructs the mind into a system of organs of computation, originally designed by natural selection to help our hunter and gatherer ancestors specifically cope with the problems of foraging for food.[47] Yet as Edelman observed (while himself arguing for a selectionist and against a strict computer point of view), in the early behavioral encounters of a perceiving animal the world does not come divided into prearranged categories. Adapting to an unlabeled universe, then, means for vertebrates with a rich nervous system that they cannot possess precise, prespecified point-to-point hard wiring and that, in general, uniquely specific connections do not exist.[48]

Unitary perceptions, instantiated in proximity-making analogies, are the consequences of the parallel activity in the brain of many different maps, each with different degrees of functional segregation, acting collectively. But while numerous brain researchers rely on conspicuous connective metaphors such as "nets" and "maps" to describe perceptual categorization, the computational theory does not satisfactorily explain how vision, anatomical structure, the nervous system, and a shifting external milieu interact to form a sustaining and sustained psychic architecture that is also fluidly developmental. A participating consciousness, like a contextualized universe, as William James and John Dewey argued, is not composed of substances but interactive events.[49]

Modern philosophy from Descartes forward quantified certainty, that discursive activity of mathematics asserting that nothing has been introduced by the actual operation of the intellect that it cannot fully identify. The claim, in brief, is that nothing is being added or subtracted, equated or changed without the mind's active warrant that no mistake either has occurred or is possible. To ensure the maintenance of exact identity, mathematical vigilance of this sort admits only a small set of valid transformations. Discursive certainty, as opposed to the proportional adjustments typical of analogy, is a matter of stating specifically how things are staying the same and how, precisely, they are being altered.[50]

The Cartesian legacy to the view that sees the mind as a general-purpose computer learning program[51] is, I believe, twofold. First, it always raises doubts in the face of ambiguity, i.e., when things are not clear and distinct.[52] This wariness, together with the application of an anatomizing method, continues even when, by their very nature, the phenomena in question (like synesthetic qualia) cannot be clear and distinct because they shade into or permeate one another. Moreover, despite his reliance on sight in determining whether something is clear and distinct or not, Descartes ignores the fact that this physiological activity also produces a nonformalizable, nonalgorithmic insight. The practice of thought is consistent with the practice of vision precisely in its elusive capacity to move, adjust, and change registers.

This neo-Cartesianism has been challenged by Howard Gardner's hypothesis that there are actually eight human intelligences, ranging from the personal to the logical, that evolved historically to help human beings cope with adaptive problems, and Paul Rozin's claim that cognitive capacities are multiple and can be extended into other domains.[53] But such exceptions do not loosen the hold of this logical system striving after completion which seeks to establish the self-sufficiency and integrity of such concepts as identity, contradiction, proof, system, and even consciousness.

Second, a debilitating Pyrrhonian skepticism accompanies the realization that the contents of the mind have somehow become transformed and that this metamorphosis cannot be completely identified and wholly articulated through measurement. Although Gödel's incompleteness theorem affirmed that no axiomatic system can ever be proven to be fully coherent and consistent from within its own rules and postulates, the attempt to eradicate undecidability continues. To obviate the resulting corrosive doubt, mathematics moved toward a sort of noetic imperialism. Measurements became so fine-grained that they "nanotechnologized" the phenomena observed, changing complex, overwhelming experiences (like those released by the sight of *Taglioni's Jewel Casket)* into fragmented microminiatures. Yet, to rephrase David Thomas's question—when making the case for the relevance of Gödel's theorem for literary postmodernist theory—what are we presupposing when we hand ourselves the critical privilege of not observing and responding tactically to the incompleteness of our own methodologies?[54] We presuppose a transcendentally positioned thinker.

I am arguing that there are machines and machines. Massive parallel processors are imbued with claims concerning the ultimate self-sufficiency of their formalist logical operations, but more aesthetic devices refute the totalizing aims of this sort of computation. Bill Viola's engulfing use of electronic media to embed viewers in destabilizing psychoactive spaces, for example, incarnates the absorbing and repelling thrusts of consciousness.[55] Stimuli pour in, forcing us to shoulder the burden of our own processes of perception by roiling what goes on below the skin. Spinning mirrors, tinkling chimes, a rush of violent images, and then preternatural quiet form themselves into mythical, spiritual, and physical landscapes. These optical and acoustical depth charges explode into situational analogies. The viewer's fleeting time and fluctuating memories are wrenched from self-absorption, becoming intermittently linked to the ephemeral and constantly interrupted trajectories of the performers.

Devoid of text, these brilliantly colored lucid images—suddenly flaring up and dying down—paradoxically alert us to the disorientations continually warping the coherence of human thought. Sensations of giddy vertigo, elicited by an unfathomable abyss, or of unbearable anguish, called up by the sight of bound and gagged mouths accompanied by low jumbled mutterings, are not merely represented but resonate inside the viewer's body. Confrontation is always permeation. In this sense, Viola's audiovisual installations—like the *sons et lumières* ecologies of Diana Thater or the undulating liquidity of Francesc Torres's struggling nudes electronically projected onto a bed of salt[56]—are viewer-activated. Such physiological intertwinings of internal with external events challenge both the separatism of quantitative rationalism and isolationist theories of the rationality of the emotions.[57]

As is true for Tony Oursler's anxiety-stimulating videos of seething, whining, or moaning women, seeing, for Viola, is more than the instrumentalized "monitoring" of a "pixelated show."[58] Each unsettling multisensory environment puts the physical in contact with the conceptual. Our entire being stops and starts as the layered montage dips in and out of focus or jarringly switches on and off. The beholder's heightened perceptual acuity reminds us of the sensuality of the intellect and of the responsive flesh lodged within visual experience.[59]

One of the characteristics of video is its malleability. As an audiovisual, time-based medium, its extensions and contractions are perfectly suited to explore the push and pull of self-awareness. Viola's procession of spellbinding imagery, drawn from the phenomenal world, possesses the fluidity of Neoplatonic emanations. No work better exemplifies the liquidity of thought and the oceanic nature of the inner realm—with its profundities and shallows—than *Stations* (figs. 82, 83).

Created in 1994, this epiphanic installation comprises five channels of video projection amplified by unnerving underwater sounds. Five cloth screens are suspended from the ceiling of an unlit gallery. Large slabs of polished black granite are placed flat on the floor touching the screens. Five life-size "swimmers"—submerged head downward—have their vertical reflections individually righted on the highly polished, tombstone-like horizontal planes. At random intervals, these ghostly bodies glide out of the frame, leaving the vacated space shadowy and silent. Suddenly the male and female figures are resurrected, taking turns in plunging back into view with a startling splash of noise and brilliant flare of light that briefly blazes in the gloom. Although visitors to the installation are aware of one another's presence through shuffling feet, intermittent glimpses, and murmurs, the prevailing blackness ensures that everyone interacts with the apparitions wavering on multiple screens alone.

In describing *Stations*, the artist commented that "an initial surface appearance of eerie, serene beauty resides over a deeper disturbing aspect of muted violence and disorder, with the disrooted, isolated, free-floating bodies evoking an eternal state between dream and death."[60] In an earlier piece, *Reflecting Pool* (1977–1980), divers were not drowned but hovered in midair above the concentric ripples of a bottomless mirroring spring

82. Bill Viola, *Stations,* 1994.

concealed within a lush forest. Like the magical artifacts trapped within Cornell's nocturnal boxes, Viola's tranquil or agitated dark water contemplatively envelops the beholder, drawing her experientially downward into the normally unseen well of consciousness.

Significantly, video plastically models mutable and nebulous primal sensations in a way that "hard" artificial intelligence systems or smart machines do not. As a "softer," unfurling technology, it constitutes a participatory medium that intersects with our own dissolving imaginings, wants, sensations of mortality and eternity. The monumental scale, undulating motion, and elemental rhythm of *Stations*'s nudes—spanning youth to age—fuse in uncanny synchronization with the ebbings and eddyings of the beholder's inner life.

Not just the present but the past, too, offers an untapped repertory of sophisticated imaging strategies demonstrating the complexities of

83. Bill Viola, *Stations,* detail of pregnant woman.

physically, mentally, emotionally, and spiritually connecting as we rise or sink beneath our own and others' surfaces. Image schemas or gestalts, according to George Lakoff, transcend the mere collection of their disparate parts. These structured wholes—like Viola's holistic installation pieces which are the joint products of the artist's and beholder's active configuration—arise from the fitting of a passing sensation to a categorizable representation.[61] A fuller understanding of the spatial arts' perennial capacity to create junctures between automatic, unconscious perceptions and conscious thought could help account for the as-yet-noncomputed subjective characteristics of the mind.

I want to add three further reflections to current discussions about the new mind. All are based on the visuality of consciousness. The world-generating power of neural nets transforms electric patterns excited in the receptor organs into internal representations. The brain, as a vast collection of systems, is constantly deploying the images that constitute our thoughts as it interacts with the body and the outside world. In between its five main sensory input sectors and three main output sectors lie the association cortices, the basal ganglia, thalamus, amygdala, limbic system cortices, limbic nuclei, brain stem, and cerebellum. Taken together, these organs hold both innate and acquired knowledge and so help us develop a visualizable self-image over time.

First, the coherence associated with self-awareness—lasting for longer or shorter periods—becomes evident not so much by invoking the Cartesian language of automata, pulleys, and now wiring, transistors, and software, but in perceiving fugitive or lasting patterns of relations. Understood in this way, consciousness becomes real only insofar as consciousness is desired or shown to itself. The practical production of a unified and graspable display of identity arises from the selective correlation of many different representations distributed over widespread areas of the brain. But this brain is also "body-minded," and feelings are just as cognitive as other percepts.[62]

I am struck, then, by how the connective neurological language of modern science finds its symbolic counterpart in the talismanic thaumaturgy of the ancient mysteries. Greco-Egyptian temple priests invoked the ineffable oneness of the divine presence through a divisible material object. This comparison is not as improbable as might first appear. It has the virtue of embedding the enigma of not-so-cerebral bonding within a Darwin-

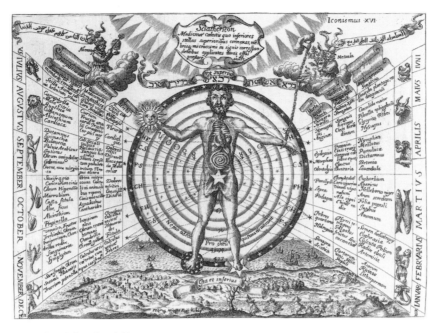

84. Athanasius Kircher, *Cosmic Man,* 1671.

ian competitive universe, riven by animal appetites and fueled by the carnal biology of natural selection.[63] Like the potent sexual attractors identified by evolutionists, the intracerebral coordination of disparate neural areas with no central faculty of thought[64] may be situated within an ancient procreative system of divination, of alluring powers and impersonal reproductive drives springing from physical attraction.

I find an uncanny similarity between the Neoplatonic cosmos of mysteriously crisscrossing forces and the technological realm of gigantic parallel distributed processors (fig. 84). This analogy is not entirely flattering. Massive parallelism posits that the billions of neurons composing the mammalian brain and woven into neural nets has no single overall point of control.[65] Obviously, there is a great deal of organization, regularity, and structure found in this system, but many of the signal processes, cognitive processes, and motor activities take place at the same time and in a quasi-automatic, unconscious way. These arrangements of matter are supposed

to have representational and causal properties: some are hard-wired or innate and others have been learned by feedback and are so strongly incorporated into us that we do not register them.[66]

Parallelism thus constructs a distributed self inside the head comprised
of a multiplicity of actions that somehow become "autopoetically"[67] coordinated. The premise that higher-level cognitive features will "emerge"
from the massively parallel interaction of basic components has a familiar
Neoplatonic ring. Moreover, this supposedly selfless self, made up of copresent hybrid elements, still seems to me to be conceived as discrete serial
singularities laid down side by side in tracks or channels. Inlaying signals is
not the same as interweaving and superimposing them within a thicketlike
matrix or rain-spattered pond.

In both the hermetic schematization of knowing and the neurocom-
puter model of cognition, all things or signaling arrays possess vertical and
horizontal linkages arcing across the three kingdoms of nature or hetero-
connecting within the somatosensory system. This new picture of a decentered mind as a disunified, heterogeneous collection of networks of
processes[68] is reminiscent of a Buddhist nondualism. But it also recalls the
demonology of the Gnostic stepped firmament where every agent is made
up of many agents. The latest, quasi-biological computers, operating according to a "production system" model, strengthen the occult comparison. But this is nothing compared to the esoteric perfecting of matter
envisioned when the futuristic fusion of the information and life sciences
finally comes around in the form of the "molecular computer," a thinking
machine made of DNA strands instead of silicon. Then, much computing
will no longer take place on the integrated circuitry of a microchip.
Equipped with synthetic molecules, memory, even a collection of reflexes
or "demons," these self-contained neurochips—like alchemical transmuta-
tions—are envisioned as sitting around magically waiting to spring to life
by automatically wiring themselves together.[69]

Synesius, Iamblichus, Proclus, and much of the late Roman world also
looked for visible omens and portents connecting the corporeal to the incorporeal domain. Mediating substances were believed to compel liaisons
between tangible objects—a stone, a gem, a piece of bone—and a higher,
intangible psychic dimension (fig. 85). These sharable artifacts were substitutes for an invisible power and summoned its hidden efficacy into a

85. *Tuscany Picture Stone.*

communal space. Leonardo restated this great theme of the geo-organism at the beginning of the sixteenth century:

By the ancients man has been called the world in miniature; and certainly this name is well bestowed, because, inasmuch as man is composed of earth, water, air and fire, his body resembles that of the earth; and as man has in him bones, the supports and framework of his flesh, the world has its rocks, the supports of the earth; as man has in him a pool of blood in which the lungs rise and fall in breathing, so the body of the earth has its ocean tide which likewise rises and falls every six hours, as if the world breathes; as in the pool of blood veins have their origin, which ramify all over the human body, so likewise the ocean sea fills the body of the earth with infinite springs of water.[70]

Not surprisingly, since there is something mysterious about the art of healing, the alliance between magic and medicine has a long history in the

86. Jan Brueghel the Younger and Adriaen Stalbemt, *The Archduke Albert and the Archduchess Isabella in a Collector's Cabinet,* c. 1620.

West. During the Renaissance, Marsilio Ficino's (1433–1499) translation of the just-discovered *Corpus Hermeticum,* as well as works by Plotinus, propagated the view that the wise physician could control disease by directing astral influences into the sick body.[71] When princely *Wunderkammern* were in their prime—beginning around the middle of the fifteenth and early sixteenth centuries—the curative and thaumaturgical properties of corals, minerals, "painted stones," ostrich eggs, tortoise shells, animal heads, musical instruments, statuary, and paintings were valued alongside their "recreative" appeal and provocative rarity (fig. 86).[72]

The usefulness of such delightful combinations of categories was predicated on the physiological bond between microcosm and macrocosm. No matter how stocked with idiosyncratic *bizarreries* many of these encrusted ebony chests appear, there is evidence for a significant amount of standardization in their contents. Hans-Olof Boström has shown the distribution of similar and, in some cases, even identical aphrodisiacs and *materia medica* across a group of *Kunstschränke* belonging to the orbit of the famous Augsburg art collector and dealer Philipp Hainhofer (active during the first third of the seventeenth century).[73] What makes the standardization of strange items (for example: rhinoceros and unicorn horns, a large bezoar, a frog cast from life) interesting from the specific standpoint of analogy— not discussed by Boström—is the fact that such anthologizing chests exhibit a general logical pattern. This cultural-normative system is erected inductively on sharable exemplary cases that help elucidate its meaning. The individual requirements of the patron or buyer are thus visibly joined to a larger social unit of interpreters, to what Dawkins called a *meme*.

I believe these curiosity cabinets embody with great power and clarity the central idea of the analogical world view, namely, that all physical phenomena, from fallen stars, to Florentine stones, to magnified fleas, to the most skillfully chased silver goblets, can be cross-referenced, linked in reconciling explanation by the informed imagination. The problem of reach they addressed is familiar from present-day computation: to see coordination across separation, that is, to couple data that is not effectively or invariably coupled by causal laws. The challenge extended by these compendious boxes, often referred to as "organisms" replete with concealed "intestines,"[74] was that they required perspicuity from the beholder as she leapt from the intricately inlaid exterior to the convoluted interior to the synoptic "precious mountain" of shells and corals heaped on top. Resembling the sumptuous, many-chambered mansion of the universe it mimicked, the opulent, multidrawered curio cabinet was an encyclopedic collection: enfolding the arts with technology, ethnography with the natural sciences, mathematical instruments with the apothecary's prophylactics, and stacking them inside a tiered container like the ascending and descending premises of an argument (see figs. 1, 65).

Rarity-stocked vitrines condensed the lavish fertility of the biological world and the inventions of humankind. This synthesizing abstraction through selection and miniaturization permits us to link a practical piece of furniture to epistemology, and pharmacological nostrums to the spectacle of nature. Enshrined marvels were thus mediating substances, unexpected symbolic and functional gifts binding the corporeal to the mental realm. As microspecimens culled from the three kingdoms of nature, the four continents, all historical epochs, and embodying every technique, they were also material objects of meditation, stimulating the search for coherence.

According to the occult tradition man has two bodies: his quintessenced sidereal self, all fire and air, and his animal self, dark as earth and water. The up-down, inner-outer dualism of this basic organization—prelapsarian heavenly flesh bound to heavy elements—suggested the possibility of manipulating terrestrial objects to make contact with the starry firmament. It was believed that one could intervene, at auspicious moments, in celestial affairs and draw down beneficial planetary effluvia into the diseased body. This medical theodicy—stretching from Böhme, Paracelsus, and Swedenborg, to George Cheyne—attempted to regain the edenic purity of fouled organs through a kind of spiritual alchemy.[75]

Talismans, amulets, charms enhanced the doctor's receptivity to stellar influences and so helped uncover elaborate sympathies correlating the corruptible with the incorruptible sphere. This mobile, interconnected universe of correspondences, predicated on the imaginative leaps of analogy, remained in place until severely compromised by the derision of the Enlightenment. The recognition of nature's ludic aspects,[76] typical of a pre-Cartesian world view, was replaced by the ideal of a grave, rational, and disciplined science. Louis de Jaucourt, in his medical articles written for Denis Diderot's and Jean Le Rond d'Alembert's *Encyclopédie* (1751–1765), scoffed at the doctrine of pictorial signatures, the belief that potent "souvenirs," or mementos from another dimension, could tie the greater to the lesser world, the internal to the external zone.

Although easy to ridicule from a rationalist standpoint, the dialectical theory of sympathies and antipathies helped viewers creatively infer how dramatically different sensory phenomena could be collected, recollected, internalized, and observed as part of their own noetic substance. While late Renaissance naturalists such as Ulisse Aldrovandi (1522–1605) delved into the secrets of a hermetic nature to discover better medicines, their baroque Jesuit counterparts, like Athanasius Kircher (1602–1680) and Filippo Buonanni (1638–1725), transformed the pleasing spectacle of a star-shot cosmos into a virtuoso technique of investigation.[77] Revealing the sportive pattern of the universe and the divinely inspired craft of its "masterpieces" demanded an artful approach from natural philosophers intent on demonstrating the profound game by which it all worked.[78]

Finding or inventing a kinship between paradoxical or difficult-to-thread-together phenomena characterized not only wonder-provoking scientific demonstrations but the playful juxtapositions of exotica with astronomical instruments (fig. 87) typical of the Kircherian Museum (1709) at the Collegio Romano, the segmented, miniature-lined compartments of a Ching dynasty treasure chest, and the fanciful leaps from the ordinary to the extraordinary stimulated by a Joseph Cornell cosmological box.

An additional aspect of this apparently global and transtemporal fascination with cabinets of curiosities is the insight they offer into the combinatorial immensity of thinkable structures. The mind, too, has been pictured as a studio, casino, grotto, art gallery, theater, treasury of rarities hold-all, coffer or encyclopedic place to fill with gems and medals (see fig. 65), peepshow or *Guckkasten* (fig. 88), *gazophylacium* or room for looking at precious objects, and literal and figurative camera obscura (see fig. 87, bottom).[79] The self as *musaeum*[80] recuperates the original meaning of its celebrated Alexandrian prototype, that academy founded by Ptolemy Philadelphus (285–247 B.C.) and dedicated to the study of the arts, sciences, and letters in combination. The fluid possession of things as well as of knowledge is inseparable from the construction of identity. Intellectual montage fights linearity by showing how all items not only are connected forward and backward over time and space but are constantly being packaged and repackaged under the pressure of different contexts. Like Vermeer's complex interior scenes showing a painter at his easel or a woman and her cavalier surprised in a moment of dalliance (fig. 89), the architecture of consciousness in the early modern period was visualized as occurring within a symbolically outfitted chamber of being.[81]

The computationalists' identification (not approximating resemblance) of the brain with consciousness, their quest for a direct link between an originating material organ and the phantasmatic presence of a singular awareness, shares in this long tradition of reclusive enclosures. What is conspicuously lacking in the scientific portrait of psychic possessions, however, is the feeling for inner space as a sanctum. There is no discernible integrating "I" ordering and combining the various faculties, modules, or intelligences that characterize the fully evolved individual.

This brings me to my second point. It seems more fruitful to situate the binding problem within the context of philosophical and rhetorical analogy than of quantitative certainty. Analogy gets at the complexly de-

87. Christophorus Scheiner, *Public and Private Jesuit Science,* 1630.

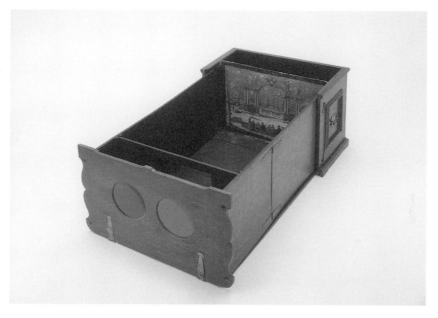

88. Anonymous, *Portable Guckkasten,* c. 1750.

signed ways in which first-person phenomena hang together better than the computer-derived "interface." Although it is not explicitly stated, cognitive science appears to be relying on the model and metaphor of an interfacial type of connectivity when it posits that the brain functions like a special sort of apparatus. According to the dictionary definition, an interface is "the collection of components which connects the analogue and digital computers to each other and controls and converts the data." As early as 1837, however, the adjective "interfacial" emerged in crystallography texts to describe the surface energy, tension, polarization, and absorption occurring between two faces of a crystal.[82] One may well ask the appropriateness, and the limiting consequences for brain research, of importing a paradigm alluding to the intercommunication either between two or more pieces of dead equipment or between the several planes of inert minerals, into the brain's organic precincts.

The nonsentient implications of this geological metaphor were extended in more recent times by Marshall McLuhan. His analysis of loud-

89. Jan Vermeer, *Young Woman with Wine Glass,*
1659–1660.

speaker telephones or electrical "intercoms" now governs, I believe, the computational notion that a whole set of confrontational systems (much like Duchamp's mechanical betrothals, Picabia's graphically sexed male and female machine-portraits produced for the pages of Stieglitz's *291*—replete with flirtatious lightbulbs, phallic spark plugs, and clock springs dipped in ink—or Rebecca Horn's darkly erotic automata) possess stream-lined components that *really do* couple in a devicelike way.[83] Norbert Wiener's military-inspired cybernetics,[84] first formulated in the 1940s, reasoning that it was similar to study living organisms or servomechanical machines (i.e., with self-correcting negative feedback), has acquired new meaning because of the recent intersection of research in molecular biology, nanoengineering, and computer science. Communications theory turned individual human beings and their biochemical systems into discrete or continuous automated messages, linguistic codes, and muffling "noise" operating within a self-regulating, closed-loop mechanism. It was not a great leap to extend this cybernetic semiotics of the body, this digital biology, into a cryptological combinatorics of the self.

But information is not intelligence, and awareness is not a response to a set of logical instructions. If it is true that human cognition is inherently modular, then it must give birth to correspondences. Analogy's efficacy consists not simply in communicating what already exists but, like consciousness, in visibly bringing forth what, in fact, it communicates. Recall that in its ability to make things actually get together, analogy resembles the affinity-producing efficacy of a charm or amulet. Generative powers of attraction—rather than the mechanistic and chance riveting of chaotic assemblages into an analytical system—belong to a magical domain of metamorphoses where imaginings take on flesh. The creative coming to-gether of opposite ideas is akin to sexual reproduction in that a third, new and unifying, concept arises from two distinct and separate sensations.

Ironically, then, this supposedly outmoded realm of corporeally conceived liaisons is more biologically up-to-date than the current model that has awareness resulting from the asexual merger of cybernetic hardware. Indeed, the joining of differences by discovering or generating similarities—whether at the macro- or microlevel—even coincides better with the fundamental premise of evolutionary theory. This posits that the earth's species, including *Homo sapiens*, arose through divergence from a common ancestor. Darwin's explanation that diversity was brought about through natural selection over millions of years is based on a principle not only for separating, but for assimilating, very different kinds of organisms. Indeed, the Genome Project is promising to link together through genetic sequencing bacteria, mice, and human beings, fundamentally altering our view of the unity of life.

Further, James Gibson's theory of ecological perception—a sensitivity to self-specifying information detectable in the ambient array—situates the organism in its experiential and cognitive environment and then seeks to discover how it learns. Although tending to ignore the physiology of perception in favor of the psychological response,[85] Gibson stresses that point of view is built into the very structure of optical awareness from earliest infancy. His assumption that all perception involves coperception of the self and the surroundings has evolutionary implications, since, for survival, all creatures must correlate the felt spatial properties of their own bodies with the seen spatial properties of others. They need to synchronize stand or flee emotions with protective movements.[86]

This emergent dimension of analogy prevents the "new mind" from being absolutely severed from the "old mind." Specifically, it succeeds in illuminating John Searle's view of sentience as a set of intricate interlocking sensations that almost pragmatically arise in the brain in response to the interactions of its many parts.[87] It also lends support to Roger Penrose's thesis that our understanding exceeds any computer because a computer uses only algorithms (that is, sets of precise rules that specify a sequence of actions to be taken in order to solve a problem or prove a proposition).[88] His position that there might be something "beyond computation" has been much attacked because, it is argued, computational cognitive science does not require that people comprehend the lengthy and incredibly complicated programs employed to solve intellectual problems.

But the issue (and here I also differ with Penrose) is not whether or not we understand the rules we use to arrive at mathematical (his example) or other conclusions but, rather, how we can be made to see or become aware of the somatic operations we undergo while we are in the process of experiencing them. As I have been suggesting, making these intricate and intuitive procedures visible constitutes the entire history of art. Moreover, by taking us back up the Darwinian ladder of evolution to the associative origins of human thought, analogy offers a nonalgorithmic technique for binding our perceptual system to our cognitive system, expressed in terms of similarities and antitheses. Learning, in this developmental scheme, does not spring from a chain of reasoning but from a dynamic back-and-forth motion among choices that embrace the entire universe in their scope.

My final point is that we are really talking about a richer, more profound view of sentience wrapped around a different type of technology. The limitation of algorithms for ascertaining what and how we know coexists with the need for a more "artful" kind of machinery analogous to the delicate logic of our thoughts. Yet even connectionism—whose adherents argue that simple networks alone account for most of thinking—has trouble with compossibility.[89] While its quasi-biological language of links and associations evokes a new theory of correspondences, this theory has difficulty explaining how meaning coming from multivariate parts is related to form an emotionally colored concept. Positing well-worn tracks in the brain, i.e., a set of linkages among nets and patterns that cooccur, still does not explain a network's individualized ability to generalize from its dense interconnectivity and superimposition of perceptions.

Emergent AL (artificial life), as Sherry Turkle proposes, is making it easier to soften the boundaries between smart artifacts and people.[90] As a decentered psychology favoring multiple identities, also typical of object-relations theorists, it is a far cry from the narrow determinism of the "hard" AI machine ideal of replication or copy. It also modulates connectionism's structuring of the mind's "software" into programs for processing rule-driven systems. But the desktop PC with which she conjures is also a newly conceived *iconic* computer. The electronic fluidity of a Macintosh, say, in contrast to robotics, presents powerful analogues to William James's stream of consciousness. Today, the joining impulses of analogy—visible on the coursing Internet—call forth an endless parade of flexible selves.

Nonetheless, it is the rococo antecedents to the hyperlinked matrix—especially the Piranesian *capriccio* predicated on analogy (fig. 90)—that most nearly resemble the unpredictable, staglike jumps of neurons. The Venetian architect's densely etched interweavings of discrete ruins, drawn from wildly different historical periods, require an equally sophisticated apprehension from the beholder. The viewer's ability to pick and choose among the accumulating remains also characterizes the discriminating Hogarthian eye, in restless pursuit of the line of beauty. Both kinds of vision enact the mind's swift hunt as it agilely leaps along global reentry pathways, darting in and out of memory, fleeing toward and away from categories.

90. Giambattista Piranesi, *Appian Way,* 1756.

Remember how Umberto Eco satirized the early-modern "excess of wonder" that drove an Agrippa of Nettesheim or an Athanasius Kircher into the mania of Hermetic semiosis encouraging the exploitation of any similarity.[91] But unlike the interpretive extremes typical of postmodern deconstructionism, the classical theory of analogy does not claim that, for the healthy mind, everything means almost anything or necessarily possesses a similarity to everything else. In fact, analogy has something specific to add to the digital revolution and to the so-called death of linear thinking.[92]

If the gauzy permeability of consciousness can be described as a "leaking rainbow,"[93] in a metaphor derived from scintillant icons and chromatic software, it is also a universal characteristic composed of shifting patterns generated by light impulses operating at top speed. The computer's nonsequential capacity to arrange data first in this way, then in that, has an important precursor in Leibniz's *ars combinatoria*. This metaphysical hieroglyphics of manipulable ciphers was simultaneously an analogical method for spurring mental invention and a parallel processing model of the abstracting powers of intelligence demonstrating that human beings can think about more than one thing at a time.

Not preestablished harmony but preestablished chaos seems to describe the constant, raindroplike, background activity of firing neurons whose multimodal oscillations await specific excitation and dynamic coupling into cell assemblies. Reminiscent of Leibniz's ecstatic *Monadology*, sentience has once again become definable as arising within self-organizing modular units that are somehow interlinked into orderly cortical communities.[94] We both solipsistically concentrate the universe within ourselves and rapturously radiate it outward to others.

In sum: it seems that the crux of the problem of consciousness lies in the flagrant contrast or clash between organ and awareness. How does one satisfactorily reconcile the paradox of a disembodied brain as a scientific conglomerate of dissected processes with the gut feelings, flickers of emotion, moral struggles, and secret attractions we intuitively feel? I have been arguing that the solution to this dilemma requires the full participation of humanistic imaging in that supposedly "interdisciplinary discipline,"[95] cognitive science.

Art constructs a tenuous point of contact between an infinite mass of precisely firing neurons and the chaos of our monadic inner atmosphere. It makes visible both the compositional hard wiring as well as the emotional cloudiness of thought colliding with recalcitrant matter. Complex artworks, themselves the incarnate demonstration of the sophisticated processes of high-order cognition, go beyond the analytical issues being tackled in neuroscience laboratories. While collage and assemblage show how information that has come into the brain is broken down into separate functions, video reveals how that information is unified in real time.

So far, nothing in chemistry, physics, or biology explains the nature of this subjective experience or captures those moments of connectedness when we most vividly sense that someone is at home inside our heads. By engaging with the full spectrum of images, we can begin to understand the qualitative range of experiences happening to different people when they behold the deep red of a sunset or are wrenched by the sight of suffering. Revitalizing forgotten or despised analogy, then, might help us discover not only how the mind seeks out and binds clear with fuzzy arrangements, or manages to synthesize the vast quantities of chaotic data with which we are increasingly inundated, but how, time and again, it stitches our mutable, compound selves into a single self in periods of consciousness.

Postscript: Beyond Duality: From Adepts to Agents

Why is the postmodern embrace of unbridgeable difference deeply problematic? I have suggested that both the intellectual and the practical emphasis on extreme otherness, added to a flat and homogeneous view of similarity as stale iteration, have resulted in an aesthetic, philosophical, ethical, and social calamity. We seem to be obsessed with identity, not recognition. At a deep level, this book has been about the limitations of separability. The question I returned to throughout these chapters was whether it was possible to reclaim a more sophisticated model of resemblance and participation. The search for common ground and avenues of reconciliation never seemed more urgent than today, when many countries are racked by ethnic or religious strife. Such a redemptive method reaffirming attentive interaction would offer diverse human beings real agency, rather than blind adherency, and so avoid the nightmare of living in unforgiving adjacencies, trapped within serial monocultures.

The repeated tracing of a trajectory of negation ends by stifling, and then deadening, the imaginative effort to connect. We observed how the German romantics reached melancholic stalemate in irony. Schlegel, Novalis, and Fichte, in their unstinting praise of the fragment as resisting incorporation, so extolled the play of perpetual construction and deconstruction that they were incapable of building anything in the end. This fundamentally mosaicizing or allegorical procedure fractured and resutured motley objects into nonrepresentational fictions. The permanently broken composites of nonmimetic disanalogy need to be reassessed not least because of the active lessons in synergy coming from evolutionary biology (continuity in change), genetics (why do organisms resemble yet differ from their parents?), developmental biology (what is responsible for shared human traits and for the uniqueness of individuals?), and organismal biology (how do living organisms relate to nonliving things?).

The Genome Project outstrips even these conjoining subjects in its pursuit of braided interaction at the cellular level. Its intention is to map all sequences and all possible relations of the three billion base pairs typically found in the genetic material in the chromosome of any particular person.[1] The rise of new, coordinated creation myths and the return of a recombinant cosmology—prompted by the interlace of hybrid DNA—suggest that human beings might start to treasure their plaited history not just as distinctive members of a specific nation, ethnic group, class, or gender, but as a boundary-straddling *species* belonging to a vast, interconnected, and ancient gene pool.

This communitarian enterprise is not to be confused with the current dubious business tactic of consolidating mergers, with virtual morphing, or with cultural erasure by appropriation. For as Maynard Olsen reminds us, every creature, like the acorn in Howard Nemerov's poem of the same title, must assemble itself using local materials.[2] This emergent biological account of continual yet fluctuating global exchange is closer to Leibniz's tightly integrated system of monads and to the anthologizing *omnium gatherum* of the collaging *Wunderkammer* which his metaphysics helped define. As a simultaneously material and immaterial transaction, the nonlinear ordering of cosmic particulars also mirrors that crisscrossing dialectic energizing the electronic collective of cyberspace.[3]

Analogy's duality-exorcising figures originated, flourished, and declined with the rise and fall of animistic cosmogonies, divination rituals, pre-Socratic philosophy, ancient rhetorical theory, and Renaissance and baroque poetics. The purpose of this two-way phenomenological process was to reflect and incarnate the ties that mysteriously bound the invisible to the visible sphere in consciousness-expanding emanations. It is not surprising that love and desire governed a viewer-oriented system of correspondences linking the known with the unknown, the near with the far, the transitory with the absolute. As a behavioral theory for defining social interaction, it summoned the imagination to invent reconciling images to stand in the merciful middle between the dichotomies of an argument, or between immanence and transcendence, or, just generally, between apparently insuperable incongruities. The presence of others in their natural or cultural activities was thus always acknowledged in this generous notion of a mutual reality.[4]

Leibniz is the iconophilic hero of these meditations. I used him to challenge the nonexistent, or at best severely limited, role assigned to information-rich images in linguistics-dominated cognitive psychology, philosophy of mind, and the history of science and technology. Considering the intense interest evinced in rhizomatic, chaotic, and hyperlinked systems, it is stunning to me that debates about the surfacing of complex order now going on at the intersection of distributed computing, molecular biology, nanotechnology, artificial intelligence, and artificial life do not draw more on the most richly intricate objects of them all: works of art. I argue that high-level imagery not only demonstrates the intelligence *in* perception, but makes us aware of the myriad ways in which we become aware. "Soft," artful machinery—like televisual video or the toolbarred personal computer—do not duplicate or replicate consciousness; rather they create evocative analogs that sensuously capture the epiphanies of first-person subjective experience.

Leibniz also foresaw the need for an ideographic combinatorics distilling all experience into a nimble hieroglyphics. The dense visual-verbal synthesis going on in cyberspace, and embodied in the popular clip art of the Web, has hastened the collapse of discrete media. Icons and texts that formerly occupied separate domains are now forcibly channeled into a single streaming multimedium composed of pixels. Leibniz's symbiotic ciphers anticipated the rapidly evolving field of visual language[5] that asks what visual and verbal elements do best and what synergistic meanings are ignited when they become integrated electronically into concentrated units of communication.

All historical disciplines are now in crisis; the history of art is no exception. But this current malaise, I think, is less about the refrain "What method do we write in?" and more about the bedrock problem of how to reinvent any backward-looking form of inquiry for the smart-machine era. How do we reconstruct the experiential quality of persons, places, acts, and events so that they might be illuminatingly recalled in and for the present? The analogical method as a metaphorics[6] can contribute substantially to the rhetorical construction of an integrated *imagistics*. Such a perspectival modeling of networks of resemblance would cut across temporal and disciplinary divides to bring back concretely what has been unfairly lost or obscured.

How, then, do we tie investigations of the premodern era to those of the contemporary scene so that each is restored to the other in its full iridescence? I have been arguing that this pressing question might usefully take the following form for the visual arts: what sorts of major issues still unite the complex analog imagery and formats of the past with dynamic database systems that fluctuate as a whole because of the information crisscrossing them? This analogical conundrum, focused on ways to craft new functions and connect persisting structures, is thwarted by Gnostic institutional splintering. In the 1960s, the study of the then newer media, like film and video, became compartmentalized within English departments. During the last decade, these now more elderly media have been forming departments of their own. Today, the exploding fields of multimedia, computer graphics, robotics—the new new media—are generally set apart within art, design, or communication schools whose main mission is to teach the evanescent moment.

As things stand, the creative and the genealogical sides of the house never meet. Yet, it seems to me, historical images should function as more than muffled "legacy" applications divorced from the vital imaging innovations blossoming all around them. Not to consider them in tandem confers on the former the status of museological mummies, perceived as irrelevant or out-of-date, and on the latter the onus of being merely fashionable commodities responding to the art-futures market. Global communication must reclaim the full revelatory gamut of unfamiliar media to serve as intelligent content and attractive format providers but, above all, to add complexity, context, and depth to volatile, thinned and rootless e-collage.

In the end, I like to think that restorative and enlivening analogy can continue to perform in the modern world much like Bruno Latour's "propositions."[7] As the name indicates, a proposition does not pertain to language, it is not a statement. Rather, it is an *offer* extended by one body or thing to another inviting it to relate in a new manner. Each entity is forced to pay attention to the other, and, in so doing, both diverge from their customary paths to venture onto territory which, although it appears foreign from each of their unique vantage points, nonetheless belongs to an interdependent existence.

The viewer's leap to understanding, to the discovery of intermediaries that are simultaneously global and localized, literally requires room to maneuver. Gaps in information help the observer realize that, no matter how intensive a particular discipline's investigation of specific phenomena might be, holes always remain in the data. These pockets of space offer opportunities for interweaving the specialized knowledge of individual cases with more general principles. In Leibnizian fashion, the seer is encouraged to raise her sights, not in order to reproduce an identical view valid for all, but to gain access over time to as many intertwined coexistent and coextensive partial aspects as possible. Analogy, I believe, can still help us see how to get from here to there.

Notes

1 Postmodernism and the Annihilation of Resemblance

1. Umberto Eco, *Interpretation and Overinterpretation: The Tanner Lectures* (with Richard Rorty, Jonathan Culler, and Christine Brooke-Rose), ed. Stefan Colline (Cambridge: Cambridge University Press, 1996).

2. Plato *Timaeus* 31c.

3. Norbert W. Mtega, *Analogy and Theological Language in the Summa contra Gentiles* (Frankfurt am Main and Bern: Peter Lang, 1984), p. 17.

4. See Gregory L. Ulmer, *Heuretics: The Logic of Invention* (Baltimore: Johns Hopkins University Press, 1994).

5. David Tracy, *The Analogical Imagination: Christian Theology and the Culture of Pluralism* (New York: Crossroad, 1981), p. 408.

6. Marjorie Perloff, *Wittgenstein's Ladder: Poetic Language and the Strangeness of the Ordinary* (Chicago: University of Chicago Press, 1996), p. 66.

7. Ole Bouman, "*Homo Significans* as Middling Class," in Ole Bouman, ed., *"And Justice for All . . ."* (Maastricht: Jan van Eyck Akademie Editions, 1994), pp. 29–30.

8. David A. Hollinger, *Postethnic America: Beyond Multiculturalism* (New York: Basic Books, 1995), p. 105.

9. Mladen Dolar, "'I Shall Be with You on Your Wedding Night': Lacan and the Uncanny," *October* 58 (1991), 16.

10. Daniel Roche, "*L'Encyclopédie* et les pratiques du savoir au XVIIIe siècle," in Roland Schaer, ed., *Tous les savoirs du monde. Encyclopédies et bibliothèques, de Sumer au XXIe siècle*, exh. cat. (Paris: Bibliothèque Nationale de France/Flammarion, 1996), p. 371.

11. Yannick Maignien and Jacques Virbel, "Encyclopédisme et hypermédias: de la difficulté d'être et la complexité du dire," in Schaer, ed., *Tous les savoirs du monde*, p. 466.

12. N. M. Swerdlow, *The Babylonian Theory of the Planets* (Princeton: Princeton University Press, 1998), pp. 2–5.

13. Michel de Coster, *L'analogie en sciences humaines* (Paris: Presses Universitaires de France, 1978), p. 47. Also see Claude Lévi-Strauss, *Anthropological Myth Lectures (1951–1982)* (Oxford: Basil Blackwell, 1987), p. 103.

14. Gilles Deleuze, *The Fold: Leibniz and the Baroque*, trans. Tom Conley (Minneapolis: University of Minnesota Press, 1993), p. 81.

15. Peter Brunette, "The Spatial Arts: An Interview with Jacques Derrida," in Peter Brunette and David Wills, eds., *Deconstruction and the Visual Arts: Art, Media, Architecture* (Cambridge: Cambridge University Press, 1994), pp. 26–28.

16. Friedrich Wilhelm Josef von Schelling, *Philosophie und Religion* (Tübingen: In der I. G. Cotta'schen Buchhandlung, 1804), pp. 6, 9.

17. Catherine Ginelli Martin, *The Ruins of Allegory: Paradise Lost and the Metamorphosis of Epic Convention* (Durham: Duke University Press, 1998), pp. 83–87.

18. Eric Miller, "Masks of Negation: Greek *eironeia* and Schegel's *Ironie*," *European Romantic Review* 8 (Fall 1997), 360–385.

19. Cited in Miller, "Masks of Negation," p. 375. I translated the German. I disagree with Miller's contention that Schlegel was able to maintain the dynamic contradiction.

20. Patricia Fara, *Sympathetic Attractions: Magnetic Practices, Beliefs, and Symbolism in Eighteenth-Century England* (Princeton: Princeton University Press, 1996), p. 174.

21. Johann Wolfgang von Goethe, *Elective Affinities*, trans. Elizabeth Mayer and Louise Bogan (Chicago: Henry Regnery, 1963), p. 40.

22. On the centrality of the fragment within the systemless system of the Jena romantics, see Azade Seyhan, "Fractal Contours: Chaos and System in the Romantic Fragment," in Richard Eldridge, ed., *Beyond Representation* (Cambridge: Cambridge University Press, 1996), pp. 135–136.

23. Thomas J. McCarthy, "'Epistolary Intercourse': Sympathy and the English Romantic Letter," *European Romantic Review* 6 (Winter 1996), 164–165.

24. C. Meiners, *Beytrag zur Geschichte der Denkart der ersten Jahrhunderte nach Christi Geburt, in einigen Betrachtungen über die Neu-Platonische Philosophie* (Leipzig: bey Weidmanns Erben und Reich, 1782), pp. 20–22, 95.

25. *Vorschlag zu einer Logik für den Enthusiasmus. Eine Zugabe zu des Herrn Prof. Leonj. Meisters in Zürch Vorlesung über die Schwärmerey* (Helmstadt: gedruckt bey Michael Gunthr Leuckart, 1776), pp. 9–11.

26. For the Second Sophistic (unconnected to the eighteenth century), see Jaś Elsner, *Imperial Rome and Christian Triumph: The Art of the Roman Empire, AD 100–450* (Oxford: Oxford University Press, 1998), pp. 4–7.

27. James Christie, *An Essay on That Earliest Species of Idolatry, the Worship of the Elements* (Norwich: Printed at the Stanhopian Press of Stevenson, Matchett, and Stevenson, 1814), p. ii.

28. Cynthia Wall, "The English Auction: Narratives of Dismantlings," *Eighteenth-Century Studies* 31 (Fall 1997), 5. Wall does not discuss Christie's esoteric interests.

29. A[nthelme Brillat-Savarin] Savarien, *Histoire des philosophes modernes avec leur portrait gravé dans le goût du crayon d'après les planches dessinées par les plus grds. peintres*, 2 vols. (2d ed., Paris: de l'Imprimerie de Brunet, 1762–1763), I, lxiv.

30. F. A. David, *Antiquités Etrusques, Grecques, et Romaines. Gravées par . . .* [with text by d'Hancarville], 5 vols. (Paris: Chez l'auteur, 1785–1787), II, 5–7.

31. Cited in M. Ouvaroff, *Essay on the Mysteries of Eleusis*, trans. J. D. Price with observations by J. Christie (London: Printed for Rodwell and Martin, 1817), p. 32.

32. See my *Body Criticism: Imaging the Unseen in Enlightenment Art and Medicine* (Cambridge, Mass.: MIT Press, 1991), especially chap. 6: "Sensing."

33. Sherry Turkle, *The Second Self: Computers and the Human Spirit* (New York: Simon & Schuster, 1984), p. 211.

34. For this unity of the senses, see Donald Hoffman, *Visual Intelligence* (New York: W. W. Norton, 1998), pp. 17–23.

35. Michael Berube, *Public Access: Literary Theory and American Cultural Politics* (London and New York: Verso, 1994), p. 206.

36. Fredric Jameson, *Signatures of the Visible* (New York and London: Routledge, 1990), p. 1.

37. For a persuasive rethinking of the Iconoclast controversy, see Marie-José Mondzain, *Image, icône, économie. Les sources byzantines de l'imagination contemporaine* (Paris: Seuil, 1996), p. 17.

38. Donald Kuspit, *Bourgeois: An Interview* (New York: Vintage Books, 1988), p. 34.

39. Margit Rowell, *Objects of Desire: The Modern Still Life*, exh. cat. (New York: Harry N. Abrams, 1997), p. 106.

40. Michael Randall, *Building Resemblance: Analogical Imagery in the Early Renaissance* (Baltimore: Johns Hopkins University Press, 1996), p. 103.

41. G. S. A. Mellin, *Encyclopädisches Worterbuch der kritischen Philosophie oder Versuch einer fasslichen und vollständige Erklärung der in Kants kritischen und dogmatischen Schriften enthaltenen Begriffe und Sätze*, 6 vols. (Zullichau and Leipzig: Bei Friedrich Frommann, 1804), I, 145, "Analogie."

42. Heather Rebstock, "Learning How Children Learn Language, " *Mosaic* 4 (Spring 1995), 1–3.

43. Frederick Crews, "The Consolation of Theosophy II," *New York Review* (October 3, 1996), pp. 38–44.

44. Alasdair MacIntyre has written eloquently about the absence of a standard or measure by which rival claims can be adjudicated in his *Three Rival Versions of Moral Enquiry* (London: Duckworth, 1990), pp. 5–8.

45. Alan Ryan, "The Politics of Dignity," *New York Review* (July 11, 1996), p. 17.

46. Francesco Romeo, *Analogie. Zu einem relationalen Wahrheitsbegriff im Recht* (Ebelsbach: Verlag Rolf Gremer, 1991), p. 41.

47. Ibid., p. 47.

48. William Ian Miller, *Humiliation and Other Essays on Honor, Social Discomfort, and Violence* (Ithaca: Cornell University Press, 1993), p. 131.

49. Isaiah Berlin, "Kant as an Unfamiliar Source of Nationalism" (1972), in Henry Hardy, ed., *The Sense of Reality: Studies in Ideas and Their History* (New York: Farrar, Straus and Giroux, 1997).

50. Judith N. Shklar, *Ordinary Vices* (Cambridge, Mass.: Harvard University Press, 1984).

51. Avishai Margalit, *The Decent Society*, trans. Naomi Goldblum (Cambridge, Mass.: Harvard University Press, 1996), p. 180.

52. For a reexamination of the importance of reasoning by analogy in the law, see Scott Brewer, "Exemplary Reasoning: Semantics, Pragmatics, and the Rational Force of Legal Argument by Analogy," *Harvard Law Review* 109 (March 1996), 923–1029.

53. Stephen Toulmin, *Cosmopolis: The Hidden Agenda of Modernity* (New York: Free Press, 1990), pp. 175, 185.

54. See Amy Gutmann and Dennis Thompson, *Democracy and Disagreement* (Cambridge, Mass.: Harvard University Press, 1997).

55. Gustav Niebuhr, "Suddenly Religious Ethicists Face a Quandary on Cloning," *New York Times* (March 1, 1997), A1, 8. See also Martha C. Nussbaum and Cass R. Sunstein, eds., *Clones and Clones: Facts and Fantasies about Human Cloning* (New York: Norton, 1998).

56. Martin Postle, *Sir Joshua Reynolds: The Subject Pictures* (Cambridge: Cambridge University Press, 1995), p. 134. For a discussion of the moment when prints became reproductive, see David Landau and Peter Parshall, *The Renaissance Print, 1470–1550* (New Haven: Yale University Press, 1994).

57. Christopher M. S. Johns, "Subversion through Historical Association: Canova's *Madame Mère* and the Politics of Napoleonic Portraiture," *Word & Image* 13 (January–March 1997), 44, 51.

58. R. C. Lewontin, "The Confusion over Cloning," *New York Review* (October 23, 1997), p. 18.

59. Hillel Schwartz, *The Culture of the Copy: Striking Likenesses, Unreasonable Facsimiles* (New York: Zone Books, 1996), p. 38.

60. On the importance of performing geometry, see Sha Xin-Wei, "Postscript (TM)? Writing in Logic, Clay, Smoke, and Chalk," paper presented at the conference on "Imaging and Visualization in the Cultures of Science and Medicine," Tanner Humanities Center, University of Utah (March 7, 1998).

61. Kevin Salatino, *Incendiary Art: The Representation of Fireworks in Early Modern Europe, Bibliographies & Dossiers* (Los Angeles: Getty Research Institute Publications and Exhibitions Program, 1997), pp. 95–97.

62. Richard Shiff, "Original Copy," *Common Knowledge* 3 (Spring 1994), 87–107.

63. Abigail Solomon-Godeau, "Suitable for Framing: The Critical Recasting of Cindy Sherman," *Parkett* 29 (1991), 112–115.

64. Amy M. Spindler, "Making the Camera Lie, Digitally and Often," *New York Times* (June 17, 1997), B8.

65. Peter Kendall, "Human Cloning Debate: Why Do It? Who'd Be Hurt? Should It Be Legal?" *Chicago Tribune* (February 23, 1997), Sect. 1, 8.

66. Stanley Rosen, *Plato's Sophist: The Drama of Original and Image* (New Haven: Yale University Press, 1983).

67. Kim A. McDonald, "Scientists Ask: What Is a Subspecies?" *Chronicle of Higher Education* (March 17, 1995), A9, 15.

68. D'Arcy Wentworth Thompson, *On Growth and Form*, ed. John Tyler Bonner (Cambridge: Cambridge University Press, 1961), pp. 15–22.

69. René Thom, *Esquisse d'une sémiophysique. Physique aristotélicienne et théorie des catastrophes* (Paris: Inter Editions, 1988), p. 223.

70. Thompson, *On Growth and Form*, pp. 268–270.

71. Stephen Jay Gould, "Darwinian Fundamentalism," *New York Review* (June 12, 1997), 34–37.

72. Stephen Jay Gould, "Evolution: The Pleasures of Pluralism," *New York Review* (June 26, 1997), 47–52.

73. Helena Cronin, *The Ant and the Peacock: Altruism and Sexual Selection from Darwin to Today* (Cambridge: Cambridge University Press, 1991), p. 8.

74. Zemir Zeki, *A Vision of the Brain* (Cambridge: Blackwell Scientific, 1993), discusses the difference between modular and hierarchical principles in the visual system, but leaves open the problem of how different kinds of analyses in the different areas are brought together to produce unified visual percepts.

75. Steven Pinker, *How the Mind Works* (New York: W. W. Norton, 1997).

76. Ellis Shookman, "Pseudo-Science, Social Fad, Literary Wonder: Johann Casper Lavater and the Art of Physiognomy," in Ellis Shookman, ed., *The Faces of Physiognomy: Interdisciplinary Approaches to Johann Casper Lavater* (Columbia, S.C.: Camden House, 1993), pp. 1–24.

77. See my *Body Criticism*, chap. 1: "Dissecting."

78. Gerald Graff, "The University *Is* Popular Culture," in Ray B. Browne and Marshall Fishwick, eds., *Preview 2001+: Popular Culture Studies in the Future* (New York: Popular Press, 1996), pp. 16–17.

79. Gerald Graff, *Beyond the Culture Wars: How Teaching the Conflicts Can Revitalize American Education* (New York: W. W. Norton, 1992), especially chaps. 6 and 9.

80. Shigemi Inaga, "The Impossible Avant-Garde in Japan: Does the Avant-Garde Exist in the Third World? Japan's Example: A Borderline Case of Misunderstanding in Aesthetic Intercultural Exchange," *Yearbook of Comparative and General Literature* 41 (1993), 67–75.

81. Dipesh Chakrabarty, "Minority Histories, Subaltern Pasts," unpublished paper (I am grateful to Professor Chakrabarty for sharing this with me).

82. Andrew Pollack, "Happy in the East (^_^) or Smiling :-) in the West," *New York Times* (August 12, 1996), C5.

83. Jon Krakauer, "To Build on the Mall, Follow the Cardinal Rules," *Smithsonian Magazine* 27 (May 1996), 76–81.

84. I coined the term in my *Voyage into Substance: Art, Nature, and the Illustrated Travel Account, 1760–1840* (Cambridge, Mass.: MIT Press, 1984), chap. 2: "The Natural Masterpiece."

85. Christopher Pearson, "Le Corbusier and the Acoustical Trope: An Investigation of Its Origins," *Journal of the Society of Architectural Historians* 56 (June 1997), 168.

86. David Shenk, *Data Smog: Surviving the Information Glut* (New York: HarperCollins, 1997).

87. See my "Think Again: The Intellectual Side of Images," *Chronicle of Higher Education* (June 20, 1997), B6–7; and "Educating Digiterati," *Art Bulletin* 79 (June 1997), 214–216.

88. Saul Hansell, "Is This an Honest Face?" *New York Times* (August 20, 1997), C1, 3.

89. Jon Ippolito, "Trusting Aesthetics to Prosthetics," *Art Journal* 56 (Fall 1997), 69–71.

90. Simon Alderson, "*Ut Pictura Poesis* and Its Discontents in Late Seventeenth and Early Eighteenth Century France," *Word & Image* 11 (July–September 1995), 256–263.

91. Peter H. Lewis, "Technology: On the Net," *New York Times* (November 3, 1997), C5.

2 Figures of Reconciliation

1. David Abram, *The Spell of the Sensuous: Perception and Language in a More-Than-Human World* (New York: Pantheon Books, 1996), pp. 26–27.

2. The surrealists, especially Breton and Dalí in their writings published between 1928 and 1930, make evident the kinship (still latent in the romantics) between mental illness and avant-garde artistic practices. See Adam Jolles, "Paranoiac Pictures and Delusional Discourse: The Surrealist Challenge to French Psychiatric Authority," *Chicago Art Journal* 8 (Spring 1998), 43–61.

3. David Howes, "Sensorial Anthropology," in David Howes, ed., *The Varieties of Sensory Experience: A Sourcebook in the Anthropology of the Senses* (Toronto: University of Toronto Press, 1991), p. 167.

4. Keith J. Holyoak and Paul Thagard, *Mental Leaps: Analogy in Creative Thought* (Cambridge, Mass.: MIT Press, 1995), p. 53.

5. Marie-Dominique Gineste, *Analogie et cognition. Etude expérimentale et simulation informatique* (Paris: Presses Universitaires de France, 1997), pp. 83–84.

6. On the German Counterenlightenment, see Jeffrey S. Librett, "Humanist Antiformalism as a Theopolitics of Race: F. H. Jacobi on Friend and Enemy," *Eighteenth-Century Studies* 32 (Winter 1998–1999), 234–235.

7. For a protracted analysis of many of Kant's early critics and the rise of metacriticism, see Frederick C. Beiser, *The Fate of Reason: German Philosophy from Kant to Fichte* (Cambridge, Mass.: Harvard University Press, 1989), pp. 43–44.

8. Enzo Melandri, *La linea e il circolo. Studio logico-filosofico sull'analogia* (Bologna: Società editrice Il Mulino, 1968), p. 64.

9. Roger Blood, review of Beiser, *The Early Political Writings of the German Romantics* (see next note), *European Romantic Review* 8 (Spring 1997), 222–223.

10. Frederick C. Beiser, ed. and trans., *The Early Political Writings of the German Romantics* (Cambridge: Cambridge University Press, 1996), p. 101.

11. Wilhelm von Humboldt, "On the Task of the Historian," in Kurt Mueller-Vollmer, ed., *The Hermeneutics Reader: Texts of the German Tradition from the Enlightenment to the Present* (New York: Columbia University Press, 1985), p. 112.

12. Thomas E. Maresca, "Personification versus Allegory," in Kevin L. Cope, ed., *Enlightening Allegory: Theory, Practice, and Contexts of Allegory in the Late Seventeenth and Eighteenth Centuries* (New York: AMS Press, 1993), p. 27.

13. For a discussion of analogical/disanalogical arguments in legal theory, see Scott Brewer, "Exemplary Reasoning: Semantics, Pragmatics, and the Rational Force of Legal Argument by Analogy," *Harvard Law Review* 109 (March 1996), 1006–1016.

14. Hazard Adams, "The Fate of Allegory," in Cope, ed., *Enlightening Allegory*, p. 13.

15. Thomas A. Vogler, "The Allegory of Allegory: Unlockeing Blake's 'Crystal Cabinet,'" in Cope, ed., *Enlightening Allegory*, pp. 77–78.

16. See Lisa Low and Anthony John Harding, eds., *Milton, the Metaphysicals, and Romanticism* (Cambridge: Cambridge University Press, 1994).

17. Sara Maza, "'Only Connect': Family Values in the Age of Sentiment: Introduction," *Eighteenth-Century Studies* 30 (Fall 1997), 209.

18. L. Bruno Puntel, *Analogie und Geschichtlichkeit. Philosophiegeschichtlich-kritischer Versuch über das Grundproblem der Metaphysik* (Freiburg: Herder, 1969), p. 10.

19. Peter Sloterdijk, *Critique of Cynical Reason*, trans. Michael Eldred (Minneapolis: University of Minnesota Press, 1987), p. 3.

20. Elena Russo, "Sociability, Cartesianism, and Nostalgia in Libertine Discourse," *Eighteenth-Century Studies* 30 (Summer 1997), 383–400.

21. Isabel G. MacCaffrey, *Spenser's Allegory: The Anatomy of Imagination* (Princeton: Princeton University Press, 1976), pp. 34–66.

22. Dorothy Koenigsberger, *Renaissance Man and Creative Thinking: A History of Concepts of Harmony, 1400–1700* (Hassocks, Sussex: Harvester Press, 1979), p. 103.

23. Leonard Barkan, *The Gods Made Flesh: Metamorphosis and the Pursuit of Paganism* (New Haven: Yale University Press, 1986), p. 39.

24. Victor I. Stoichita, *L'instauration du tableau* (Paris: Meridens-Klinksieck, 1993), pp. 271–272.

25. Sir Joshua Reynolds, *The Literary Works* (London: T. Cadell and W. Davies, 1819), pp. 3, 97.

26. Karen Lang, "The Dialectics of Decay: Rereading the Kantian Subject," *Art Bulletin* 79 (September 1997), 427.

27. Birgit Recki, "'Ideal der Schönheit' und Primat der Natur. Zur systematischen Interpretation des ästhetischen Gefühls," in *Proceedings of the Eighth International Kant Congress*, Memphis, 1995 (Milwaukee: Marquette University Press, 1995), II, 473.

28. Gilles Deleuze, *Kant's Critical Philosophy: The Doctrine of the Faculties*, trans. Hugh Tomlinson and Barbara Habberjam (Minneapolis: University of Minnesota Press, 1984), p. xii.

29. John J. Ciofalo, "Goya's Enlightenment Protagonist—A Quixotic Dreamer of Reason," *Eighteenth-Century Studies* 30 (Summer 1997), 422.

30. See Birgit Recki, "Das Gute am Schönen. Über einen Grundgedanken in Kants Ästhetik," in *Zeitschrift für Ästhetik und allgemeine Kunstwissenschaft* 37, special issue (1992), p. 22, for Kant's affinity formula, linking aesthetic to moral feeling.

31. For Kant's attempt to bind the perspectives of critical and practical reason in the earlier critiques, see Birgit Recki, "'Was darf ich hoffen?' Ästhetik und

Ethik im anthropologischen Verständnis bei Immanuel Kant," *Allgemeine Zeitschrift für Philosophie* 19, no. 1 (1994), 3–5.

32. Drew Harrison, "Hypermedia as Art System," *Art Journal* 56 (Fall 1997), p. 58.

33. See the illustration in *The Presence of Touch*, exh. cat. (Chicago: School of the Art Institute, Department of Fiber, 1996), p. 20.

34. Holyoak and Thagard, *Mental Leaps*, p. 13.

35. Claire Le Jeune, "L'outrage poétique du symbole. Diabolon et sumbolon," *Le signe, le symbole et le sacré. Cahiers internationaux* 77–79 (1994), 141.

36. Jean-François Billeter, *The Chinese Art of Writing* (New York: Rizzoli, 1990), pp. 20–21.

37. See my *Body Criticism: Imaging the Unseen in Enlightenment Art and Medicine* (Cambridge, Mass.: MIT Press, 1991), p. 449.

38. Illustrated in *The Presence of Touch*, p. 22.

39. For the importance of analogical thinking in getting beyond Samuel Huntington's "clash of civilizations" model in the conduct of foreign affairs, see Brantly Womack, "The Brightest House: Civilization and Asymmetry" (unpublished essay).

40. Arno Anzenbacher, *Analogie und Systemgeschichte* (Vienna and Munich: R. Oldenbourg Verlag, 1978), p. 74. Also see Puntel, *Analogie und Geschichtlichkeit*, p. 16. The reference is to Aquinas, *De veritate*, q. 2, a. 11.

41. David Burrell, *Analogy and Philosophical Language* (New Haven: Yale University Press, 1973), pp. 9–10, 13–18.

42. Bonnie Shulman, "What If We Changed Our Axioms? A Feminist Inquiry into the Foundations of Mathematics," *Configurations* 4 (Fall 1996), 429.

43. A. S. Byatt, *The Virgin in the Garden* (New York: Vintage, 1992), pp. 27–28.

44. Anne A. Davenport, "The Catholics, the Cathars, and the Concept of Infinity in the Thirteenth Century," *Isis* 88 (June 1997), 265–268.

45. Burrell, *Analogy and Philosophical Language*, p. 116.

46. Janet Zweig, "Ars Combinatoria: Mystical Systems, Procedural Art, and the Computer," *Art Journal* 56 (Fall 1997), 22–23.

47. Norbert W. Mtega, *Analogy and Theological Language in the Summa contra Gentiles* (Frankfurt am Main: Peter Lang, 1984), p. 22.

48. Byatt, *Virgin in the Garden*, p. 63.

49. *Ellsworth Kelly*, exh. guide (London: Tate Gallery, 1997).

50. A. S. Byatt, *The Shadow of the Sun* (San Diego: Harcourt Brace, 1993), preface, p. xiii.

51. Quoted in Jeffrey J. Kripal, *Kali's Child: The Mystical and the Erotic in the Life and Teachings of Ramakrishna* (Chicago: University of Chicago Press, 1995), p. 62.

52.   Byatt, *Virgin in the Garden*, pp. 104, 99.

53.   Dale Jacquette, ed., *Schopenhauer, Philosophy, and the Arts* (Cambridge: Cambridge University Press, 1996), p. 11.

54.   Burrell, *Analogy and Philosophical Language*, p. 41.

55.   Julian Young, "Schopenhauer, Heidegger, Art, and the Will," in Jacquette, ed., *Schopenhauer, Philosophy, and the Arts*, p. 168.

56.   Anzenbacher, *Analogie und Systemgeschichte*, pp. 74–81.

3   The Magic of Amorous Attraction

1.   On the sexual metaphors of weaving, see John Scheid and Jesper Svenbro, *The Craft of Zeus: Myths of Weaving and Fabric* (Cambridge, Mass.: Harvard University Press, 1996), p. 88.

2.   Jaś Elsner, *Art and the Roman Viewer: The Transformation of Art from the Pagan World to Christianity* (Cambridge: Cambridge University Press, 1995), p. 21.

3.   Jaś Elsner, *Imperial Rome and Christian Triumph: The Art of the Roman Empire, AD 100–450* (Oxford: Oxford University Press, 1998), p. 223.

4.   René Roques, *L'univers dionysien. Structure hiérarchique du monde selon le Pseudo-Denys* (Paris: Aubier Editions Montaigne, 1954), p. 29.

5.   Genetic criticism arose in the field of French literary research in the 1970s as a reaction to the textual closure of structuralism. See Almuth Gresillon, "Slow: Work in Progress," *Word & Image* 13 (April–June 1997), 106. I am referring to its initial cosmological appearance that also valued the dynamic over the static.

6.   See my *Body Criticism: Imaging the Unseen in Enlightenment Art and Medicine* (Cambridge, Mass.: MIT Press, 1991), chap. 3: "Conceiving."

7.   James M. Robinson, "Very Goddess and Very Man: Jesus' Better Self," in Karen L. King, ed., *Images of the Feminine in Gnosticism* (Philadelphia: Fortress Press, 1988), p. 117.

8.   Edward O. Wilson, "Back from Chaos," *Atlantic Monthly* (March 1998), pp. 41–62.

9.   Paul Grenet, *Les origines de l'analogie philosophique dans les dialogues de Platon* (Paris: Editions contemporains Boivin & Cie., 1948), p. 40.

10.   Ibid., p. 49.

11.   Andrew Benjamin, *Art, Mimesis and the Avant-Garde: Aspects of a Philosophy of Difference* (London and New York: Routledge, 1991), p. 29.

12.   Stephen Bann, *The Clothing of Clio: A Study of the Representation of History in Nineteenth Century Britain and France* (Cambridge: Cambridge University Press, 1984), p. 3.

13.   Grenet, *Les origines de l'analogie*, p. 53.

14. Plato, *Statesman*, 277d.

15. Allen Megill's *Prophets of Extremity* (Berkeley and Los Angeles: University of California Press, 1985) discusses Nietzsche, Heidegger, Foucault, and Derrida as the originators of crisis-of-meaning thinking.

16. James Francis Anderson, *Bond of Being: An Essay on Analogy and Existence* (St. Louis: Herder Book Co., 1949), pp. 135–136.

17. Marshall McLuhan, *Understanding Media: The Extensions of Man* (New York: McGraw-Hill, 1965), pp. 25–26.

18. Proclus, *Elements of Theology* 210.16–19. Also see *Commentary on the Timaeus* 1.198.9–24.

19. Enzo Melandri, *La linea e il circolo. Studio logico-filosofico sull'analogia* (Bologna: Società editrice Il Mulino, 1968), p. 67.

20. Grenet, *Les origines de l'analogie*, p. 195.

21. Deirdre Good, "Gender and Generation: Observations on Coptic Terminology with Particular Attention to Valentinian," in King, ed., *Images of the Feminine in Gnosticism*, p. 25.

22. Morris Eaves, *The Counter-Arts Conspiracy: Art and Industry in the Age of Blake* (Ithaca: Cornell University Press, 1992), p. 110.

23. Elaine Pagels, "Pursuing the Spiritual Eve: Imagery and Hermeneutics in the Hypostasis of the Archons and the Gospel of Philip," in King, ed., *Images of the Feminine in Gnosticism*, p. 188.

24. Margaret R. Miles, *Carnal Knowing: Female Nakedness and Religious Meaning in the Christian West* (Boston: Beacon Press, 1989), p. 35.

25. Genesis 2:24–25.

26. Elaine Pagels, "Adam and the Serpent in Genesis 1–3, " in King, ed., *Images of the Feminine in Gnosticism*, pp. 413–414.

27. Pagels, "Pursuing the Spiritual Eve," pp. 199–200.

28. Miles, *Carnal Knowing*, pp. 153–154.

29. Ibid., p. 203.

30. Chariton of Aphrodisias, *Kallirhoe*, ed. Karl Plepelits (Stuttgart: Anton Hiersemann, 1976), p. viii.

31. Madeleine Scopello, "Jewish and Greek Heroines in the Nag Hammadi Library," in King, ed., *Images of the Feminine in Gnosticism*, pp. 78–80.

32. For another instance in this pattern of deliberate misdescription, note Diderot's inaccurate account of Poussin's *Landscape with a Man Killed by a Snake* in the Salon of 1767. See Walter E. Rex, "The Landscape Demythologized: From Poussin's Serpents to Fénelon's 'Shades,' and Diderot's Ghost," *Eighteenth-Century Studies* 30 (Summer 1997), 412–413.

33. Mary D. Sheriff, *Fragonard: Art and Eroticism* (Chicago: University of Chicago Press, 1990), pp. 32–33.

34. Jaś Elsner, "Pausanias: A Greek Pilgrim in the Roman World," *Past and Present* 135 (1992), 5.

35. See my *Body Criticism*, pp. 387–389.

36. Kurt Rudolph, "A Response to 'The Holy Spirit is a Double Name,'" in King, ed., *Images of the Feminine in Gnosticism*, p. 235.

37. Jorunn Jacobsen Buckley, "'The Holy Spirit is a Double Name': Holy Spirit, Mary and Sophia in the Gospel of Philip," in King, ed., *Images of the Feminine in Gnosticism*, p. 212.

38. Jeffrey J. Kripal, *Kali's Child: The Mystical and the Erotic in the Life and Teachings of Ramakrishna* (Chicago: University of Chicago Press, 1995), p. 117.

39. Salvatore Cariati and Vincenzo Cicero, *To metaphorichon. Una interpretazione della definizione aristotelica della metafora* (Ferrara: Gabriele Corbo Editore, 1992), pp. viii–ix.

40. Peter T. Struck, "Against Mimesis: The Development of a Talismanic Theory of Signification in Ancient Literary Theory," Ph.D. dissertation, University of Chicago, 1997.

41. Aristotle *Topics* 2.12.105a13.

42. Aristotle *Prior Analytics* 2.23.68b15; 27.

43. A. W. Heinrich Langheim, *Das Prinzip der Analogie als juristische Methode. Ein Beitrag zur Geschichte der methodologischen Grundlagenforschung vom ausgehenden 18. bis zum 20. Jahrhunderts* (Berlin: Duncker & Humblot, 1992), p. 26.

44. Edward O. Wilson, *Consilience: The Unity of Knowledge* (New York: Alfred A. Knopf, 1998), p. 39.

45. Harold Hoeffding, *A History of Modern Philosophy*, vol. 1 (New York: Dover, 1955), pp. 195, 198–200.

46. Anthony Synnott, "Puzzling over the Senses: From Plato to Marx," in David Howes, ed., *The Varieties of Sensory Experience: A Sourcebook in the Anthropology of the Senses* (Toronto: University of Toronto Press, 1991), p. 66. Also see Aquinas, *Summa contra Gentiles*, book 3, part 1, chaps. 60, 51.

47. Miles, *Carnal Knowing*, pp. 36, 154.

48. See Marie-José Mondzain, *Image, icône, économie. Les sources byzantines de l'imagination contemporaine* (Paris: Seuil, 1996), esp. pp. 110–117, on Byzantine iconoclasm and the various ways of capturing a nonobjective reality in a graphic configuration.

49. Richard A. Grusin, *Transcendental Hermeneutics: Institutional Authority and the Higher Criticism of the Bible* (Durham: Duke University Press, 1991), pp. 15–17.

50. Norbert Mtega, *Analogy and Theological Language in the Summa contra Gentiles* (Frankfurt am Main and Bern: Peter Lang, 1984), pp. 19, 49.

51. Norbert Ernst, *Die Tiefe des Seins. Eine Untersuchung zum Ort der Analogia Entis im Denken Paul Tillichs* (Fulda: EOS Verlag, Erzabtei St. Ottilien, 1988), pp. 7–12.

52. Ibid., pp. 20–21.

53. Ibid., p. 24.

54. Benjamin, *Art, Mimesis and the Avant-Garde*, p. 182.

55. Ibid., pp. 150–152.

56. Cited in Giancarlo Maiorino, *The Cornucopian Mind and the Baroque Unity of the Arts* (University Park: Pennsylvania State University Press, 1990), p. 102.

57. Mitchell B. Merback, "Torture and Teaching: The Reception of Lucas Cranach the Elder's Martyrdom of the Twelve Apostles in the Protestant Era," *Art Journal* 57 (Spring 1998), 14–23.

58. Hans Hollaender, "Nautilus mirabilis," *Aachener Kunstblätter*, special issue (1998), pp. 461–464. Also see the exhaustive study on the nautilus shell by Hanns-Ulrich Mette, *Der Nautiluspokal. Wie Kunst und Natur miteinander spielen* (Munich and Berlin: Klinkhardt & Biermann, 1995).

59. See my *Artful Science: Enlightenment Entertainment and the Eclipse of Visual Education* (Cambridge, Mass.: MIT Press, 1994), especially chap. 1: "The Mind's Release."

60. On the technological hybrid genre, see Bruno Latour, *Aramis, or the Love of Technology*, trans. Catherine Porter (Cambridge, Mass.: Harvard University Press, 1996), pp. ix–x.

61. For Leibniz's interest in cryptography and algebra, see Pater Pesic, "Secrets, Symbols, and Systems: Parallels between Cryptanalysis and Algebra, 1580–1700," *Isis* 88 (December 1977), 677–678, 690–692.

62. On Descartes, see Diederick Raven, "The Enculturation of Logical Practice," *Configurations* 4 (Fall 1996), 400.

63. Seymour Papert, *The Connected Family: Bridging the Digital Generation Gap* (Atlanta: Longstreet Press, 1996), pp. 69–70.

64. Anderson, *Bond of Being*, pp. 149–150.

65. Gottfried Wilhelm Freiherr von Leibniz, *The Monadology*, in *Leibniz Selections*, ed. Philip P. Wiener (New York: Charles Scribner's Sons, 1951), sect. 47, p. 542.

66. Ibid.

67. Ibid., sects. 56, 57, p. 544.

68. Thomas Nickles, "Kuhn, Historical Philosophy of Science, and Case-Based Reasoning," *Configurations* 6 (Winter 1998), 78.

69. Gilles Deleuze, *The Fold: Leibniz and the Baroque*, trans. Tom Conley (Minneapolis: University of Minnesota Press, 1993), p. 60.

70. Gottfried Wilhelm von Leibniz, *New Essays on Human Understanding*, trans. Peter Remnant and Jonathan Bennett (Cambridge: Cambridge University Press, 1981), p. 376.

71. This is Brunschvicq's term, cited in Melandri, *La linea e il circolo*, p. 25.

72. This is evident even in his earliest work written in opposition to Crusius. See Immanuel Kant, *Versuch über den Begriff des negativen Grössen in die Weltweisheit einzuführen* (Königsberg: bey Johann Jacob Kantner, 1763), pp. 68–69.

73. Gottfried Wilhelm von Leibniz, *Theodicy, Abridged*, ed. Diogenes Allen, trans. E. M. Huggard (Indianapolis: Bobbs-Merrill, 1966), sect. V, p. 517. Alexander Gottlieb Baumgarten derives this notion from Leibniz and uses it in his *Aesthetica* (1750) but, I contend, without attempting to make it a part of the beauty of the system itself. On Baumgarten, see Hans Reiss, "The Rise of Aesthetics: Baumgarten's Radical Innovation and Kant's Response," *British Journal for Eighteenth-Century Studies* 20 (Spring 1997), 57.

74. Leibniz, *Monadology*, sect. 9, p. 534.

75. David L. Wheeler, "A Molecule Offers Clues to the Evolution of Vision," *Chronicle of Higher Education* (August 1, 1997), A13.

76. John Gage, *George Field and His Circle: From Romanticism to the Pre-Raphaelite Brotherhood*, exh. cat. (Cambridge: Fitzwilliam Museum, 1989), p. 7.

77. George Field, *Chromatics; or the Analogy, Harmony, and Philosophy of Colours* (1817; 3d, rev. ed., London: David Bogue, 1845), p. vii.

78. Ibid., pp. 8–10.

79. Ibid., p. 66.

80. David Hume, *A Treatise of Human Nature* (1739–1740), I.1, 2, in Charles W. Hendel, Jr., ed., *Hume Selections* (New York: Charles Scribner's Sons, 1955), pp. 13–14.

81. Friedrich Nietzsche, *The Gay Science* (1882), in *The Portable Nietzsche*, ed. Walter Kaufmann (New York: Viking, 1954), aphorism 341, pp. 101–102.

82. Valerio Valeri, "Constitutive History: Genealogy and Narrative in the Legitimation of Hawaiian Kingship," in Emiko Ohnuki-Tierney, ed., *Culture through Time: Anthropological Approaches* (Stanford: Stanford University Press, 1990), p. 160.

83. James Lingwood, "Different Times," in *The Epic and the Everyday: Contemporary Photographic Art*, exh. cat. (London: South Bank Centre, 1994), pp. 9–10.

84. David Tracy, *The Analogical Imagination: Christian Theology and the Culture of Pluralism* (New York: Crossroad, 1981), p. 409.

85. Jeff Wall, "Muybridge's Horse," lecture, Getty Research Institute (April 30, 1998).

86. Francis Bacon, *Novum Organum*, i.10, 50.5–7.

87. Dave Hickey, "Lost Boys," in *Air Guitar: Essays on Art and Democracy* (Los Angeles: Art Issues Press, 1997), pp. 176–177.

4 Recombinancy: Binding the Computational "New Mind" to the Combinatorial "Old Mind"

1. See, for example, Peter Baumgartner and Sabine Payn, eds., *Speaking Minds: Interviews with Twenty Cognitive Scientists* (Princeton: Princeton University Press, 1995), p. 11.

2. Steven Mithen, *The Prehistory of the Mind: The Cognitive Origins of Art, Religion and Science* (London: Thames and Hudson, 1997).

3. For a discussion of Jerome Bruner's *The Culture of Education*, see Sharon Helmer Poggenpohl, "Doubly Damned: Rhetorical and Visual," unpublished essay, 1998, pp. 7–8.

4. The Göttingen Neurobiology Conferences have led the way in integrating the *history* of the neurosciences with cognitive neuroscience. See, for example, Norbert Elsner and Heinz Wässle, eds., *From Membrane to Mind: Proceedings of the 25th Göttingen Neurobiology Conference 1997* (Stuttgart: Georg Thieme Verlag, 1997), I, 469–470; and Gebhard Rusch, Siegfried J. Schmidt, and Olaf Breidbach, eds., *Interne Repräsentationen. Neue Konzepte der Hirnforschung* (Delfin: Suhrkamp, 1996).

5. Christian Boltanski, "Discussion of Recent Work," lecture at the University of Chicago, February 24, 1998.

6. Karl Clausberg, "Endocalypse Now! Physik, Phantasie und Kunstgeschichte in der 'Dekade des Gehirns'," in Wolfgang Kersten, ed., *Radical Art History. Internationale Anthologie. Subject O. K. Werckmeister* (Zurich: ZIP, 1997), pp. 56–97.

7. Olaf Breidbach and Ernst Florey, *Das Gehirn—Organ der Seele? Zur Ideengeschichte der Neurobiologie* (Bonn: Akademie Verlag, 1993), pp. vii–xiii; and Olaf Breidbach, "Neuronaler Ästhetik—Hirnbilder und Menschenbilder," *Spiel: Siegener Periodicum zur Internationalen Empirischen Literaturwissenschaft* 12, no. 2 (1993), 302–306.

8. Olaf Breidbach, "Der Innenraum des Schädels und der Aussenraum der Welt," in Hans Rudi Fischer, ed., *Die Wirklichkeit des Konstruktivismus. Zur Auseinandersetzung um ein neues Paradigma* (Heidelberg: Carl-Auer-Systeme Verlag, 1995), pp. 309–323.

9. This point is made by Henry Plotkin, *Evolution in Mind: An Introduction to Evolutionary Psychology* (Cambridge, Mass.: Harvard University Press, 1998), p. 66.

10. Olaf Breidbach, "Interne Repräsentationen—Über die 'Welt'-generierungs-eigenschaften des Nervengewebes. Prolegomena zu einer Neurosemantik," in Axel Ziemke and Olaf Breidbach, eds., *Repräsentationismus—Was sonst?* (Braunschweig: Vieweg, 1996), pp. 176–195. See also Olaf Breidbach, "Innere Repräsentationen—oder: Träume ich meine Welt?," in Michael Fehr, Clemens Krümmel, and Markus Müller, eds., *Platons Höhle. Das Museum und die elektronischen Medien* (Cologne: Wienand Verlag, 1995), pp. 212–215.

11. F. J. Radermacher, "Cognition in Systems," *Cybernetics and Systems: An International Journal* 27 (1996), 17.

12. Klaus Holthausen and Olaf Breidbach, "Self-Organized Feature Maps and Information Theory," *Network: Computational Neural Systems* 8 (1997), 215.

13. Steven S. Pinker, *How the Mind Works* (New York: W. W. Norton, 1997), p. 564.

14. David Summers, "Real Metaphor: Towards a Redefinition of the 'Conceptual' Image," in Norman Bryson, Michael Ann Holly, and Keith Moxey, eds., *Visual Theory: Painting and Interpretation* (Cambridge: Polity Press, 1991), p. 241.

15. In his *Rewriting the Soul: Multiple Personality and the Sciences of Memory* (Princeton: Princeton University Press, 1995), Ian Hacking has tracked the existence of the soul by tracking the invention and diagnosis of multiple personality disorders (MPD) and the problem of false memory. My interest lies specifically with consciousness.

16. Francis Crick, *The Astonishing Hypothesis: The Scientific Search for the Soul* (New York: Charles Scribner's Sons, 1994), pp. 35–37.

17. Research on this is being conducted by Semir Zeki, cited in Ann Marie Seward Barry, *Visual Intelligence: Perception, Image, and Manipulation in Visual Communication* (Albany: State University of New York Press, 1997), p. 24.

18. Ibid., p. 9.

19. Owen J. Flanagan, *Consciousness Reconsidered* (Cambridge, Mass.: MIT Press, 1992), p. 102.

20. On Barwise's and Etchemendy's theory of heterogeneous logic, based on their experience with Turing's and Tarski's World applications, see William Sterner, "Logical Meaning Creation in Human-Computer Interactions," report for BioQUESTU Educational Software Consortium.

21. Semir Zeki, "Art and the Brain," *Daedalus*, 127 (Spring 1998), 82. For the schema that differentiates two cortical visual systems, one for spatial vision (a dorsal pathway from striate cortex) and one for object vision (a ventral pathway from striate cortex), see Charles G. Gross, *Brain, Vision, Memory: Tales in the History of Neuroscience* (Cambridge, Mass.: MIT Press, 1998), pp. 204–207.

22. Brian Cantwell Smith, *On the Origin of Objects* (Cambridge, Mass.: MIT Press, 1998), p. 117.

23. Jennifer Pap, "'*Entre quatre murs*': Reverdy, Cubism, and the Space of Still Life," *Word & Image* 12 (April–June 1996), 181.

24. Daniel C. Dennett, "Foreword to Robert French, *The Subtlety of Sameness*," in *Brain Children: Essays on Designing Minds* (Cambridge, Mass.: MIT Press, 1998), p. 245.

25. Stanley J. Scott, *Frontiers of Consciousness: Interdisciplinary Studies in American Philosophy and Poetry* (New York: Fordham University Press, 1991), pp. 29–30.

26. Sandra B. Rosenthal, "Pragmatic Experimentalism and the Derivation of the Categories," in Jacqueline Brunning and Paul Forster, eds., *The Rule of Reason: The Philosophy of Charles Sanders Peirce* (Toronto: University of Toronto Press, 1997), p. 130.

27. Alan Ryan, *John Dewey and the High Tide of American Liberalism* (New York: W. W. Norton, 1997), pp. 5–6. On continuity and sharing experience in Dewey, also see Richard Rorty, *Truth and Progress: Philosophical Papers* (Cambridge: Cambridge University Press, 1998), pp. 294–298.

28. Robert L. Solso, *Cognition and the Visual Arts* (Cambridge, Mass.: MIT Press, 1994), p. 99.

29. Suzanne Anker, *Gene Culture: Molecular Metaphor in Visual Art*, exh. cat. (New York: Plaza Gallery, 1994), p. 2.

30. Ken Gonzales-Day, "Hannah Höch," review of exhibition at Los Angeles County Museum of Art, June 26–September 14, 1997, *Art Issues* 50 (Summer 1997), 39.

31. Roni Feinstein, "Rauschenberg: Solutions for a Small Planet," *Art in America* 86 (February 1998), 70–71.

32. See Walter Hopps and Susan Davidson, *Robert Rauschenberg: A Retrospective*, exh. cat. (New York: Guggenheim Museum/Abrams, 1997).

33. Robert Rindler, "To Be Seduced by Technology," in *Techno-Seduction*, exh. cat. (New York: Cooper Union, 1997).

34. Walter Hopps, "Boxes," *Art International* 111 (March 20, 1964), 38.

35. Citation from the notes in the *Green Box*, dating between 1912 and 1914 but published only in 1934, quoted in Charles A. Cramer, "Duchamp from Syntax to Bride: sa langue dans sa joue," *Word & Image* 13 (July–September 1997), 282.

36. Ibid., pp. 288–289.

37. David Scott, "The Poetics of the Rebus: Word, Image, and the Dynamics of Reading in the Poster of the 1920s and 1930s," *Word & Image* 13 (July–September 1997), 270–271.

38. Donlyn Lyndon and Charles W. Moore, *Chambers for a Memory Palace* (Cambridge, Mass.: MIT Press, 1994), p. xi.

39. Ann Blair, *The Theater of Nature: Jean Bodin and the Renaissance* (Princeton: Princeton University Press, 1997), p. 156.

40. Jonathan D. Spence, *The Memory Palace of Matteo Ricci* (New York: Viking, 1984), pp. 7–8.

41. Dore Ashton, *A Joseph Cornell Album* (New York: Viking Press, 1974), pp. 4, 8, 15.

42. Daniel Schacter, *Searching for Memory: The Brain, the Mind, and the Past* (New York: Basic Books, 1996).

43. Alex Migelon and Norman Laliberte, *Art in Boxes* (New York: Van Nostrand Reinhold, 1974), p. 84.

44. Gerald M. Edelman, *Bright Air, Brilliant Fire: On the Matter of the Mind* (New York: Basic Books, 1991), p. 140.

45. Daniel C. Dennett, *Darwin's Dangerous Idea: Evolution and the Meaning of Life* (New York: Simon & Schuster, 1995), p. 520.

46. Paul M. Churchland, *The Engine of Reason, the Seat of the Soul: A Philosophical Journey into the Brain* (Cambridge, Mass.: MIT Press, 1995), p. 11.

47. Pinker, *How the Mind Works*, p. x.

48. Gerald M. Edelman, *The Remembered Present: A Biological Theory of Consciousness* (New York: Basic Books, 1989), p. 41.

49. Scott, *Frontiers of Consciousness*, pp. 74–75, 99.

50. Carl Page, "Symbolic Mathematics and the Intellect Militant: Modern Philosophy's Revolutionary Spirit," *Journal of the History of Ideas* 57 (April 1996), p. 238.

51. Owen J. Flanagan, *The Science of the Mind* (Cambridge, Mass.: MIT Press, 1984), p. 5, notes that the hydraulics-automaton model of the mind has much in common with cognitive science feedback loops, memory cores, and information processing.

52. For the connection between Descartes's epistemology and the mathematized New Science of Copernicus and Galileo, see Page, "Symbolic Mathematics and the Intellect Militant," pp. 236–237. For Descartes's difficulty in connecting the union of the mind and body with sensation, see Marleen Rozemond, *Descartes's Dualism* (Cambridge, Mass.: Harvard University Press, 1998), pp. 174–175.

53. Howard Gardner, "Thinking about Thinking," *New York Review* (October 9, 1997), 24–25; and Paul Rozin, *Basic Psychology* (New York: W. W. Norton, 1997).

54. David Wayne Thomas, "Gödel's Theorem and Postmodern Theory," *PMLA* 110 (March 1995), 252–253.

55. Marilyn A. Zeitlin, *Bill Viola: Buried Secrets*, exh. cat. (Tempe: Arizona State University Art Museum, 1996), p. 9.

56. Francesc Torres, *La furia de los santos*, exh. cat. (Granada: Diputación Provincial de Granada, Palacio de los Condes de Gabia, 1997–1998), n.p.

57. Ronald de Sousa, *The Rationality of Emotion* (Cambridge, Mass.: MIT Press, 1987), p. 28.

58. Churchland, *Engine of Reason*, p. 8.

59. Bill Viola, *Reasons for Knocking at an Empty House: Writings 1973–1994* (Cambridge, Mass.: MIT Press; London: Anthony d'Offay Gallery, 1995), p. 265.

60. *Bill Viola: Stations (1994)*, exh. handout (Los Angeles: Lannan Foundation, July 10–December 22, 1996).

61. George Lakoff, *Women, Fire and Dangerous Things: What Categories Reveal about the Mind* (Chicago: University of Chicago Press, 1987), p. 272.

62. Antonio R. Damasio, *Descartes' Error: Emotion, Reason, and the Human Brain* (New York: G. P. Putnam's Sons, 1994), pp. xv, 223.

63. George L. Hersey, *The Evolution of Allure: Sexual Selection from the Medici Venus to the Incredible Hulk* (Cambridge, Mass.: MIT Press, 1996), p. 5.

64. Flanagan, *Consciousness Reconsidered*, pp. 39–40.

65. Radermacher, "Cognition in Systems," p. 20.

66. Solso, *Cognition and the Visual Arts*, p. 39.

67. For a discussion of Maturana's and Varela's theory of autopoiesis, or the self-organization of biotic, not just abiotic, systems, see Hans R. Fischer, ed., *Autopoiesis. Eine Theorie im Brennpunkt der Kritik* (Heidelberg: Carl-Auer-Systeme Verlag, 1991), pp. 187–197.

68. Francisco J. Varela, Evan Thompson, and Eleanor Rosch, *The Embodied Mind: Cognitive Science and Human Experience* (Cambridge, Mass.: MIT Press, 1993), p. 107.

69. Pinker, *How the Mind Works*, p. 69. See also Gareth Roberts, *The Mirror of Alchemy: Alchemical Ideas and Images in Manuscripts and Books from Antiquity to the Seventeenth Century*, exh. cat. (London: British Library, 1994), pp. 65–66.

70. *The Literary Works of Leonardo da Vinci*, trans. Jean Paul Richter, 2 vols. (London: Oxford University Press, 1939), II, 929.

71. Martha Baldwin, "Abracadabra or Magic in Medicine, " in *Abracadabra: The Magic of Medicine*, exh. cat. (London: Wellcome Institute for the History of Medicine, 1996), pp. 12–13.

72. Giuseppe Olmi, "Théâtres du monde. Les collections européennes des XVIIe et XVIIe siècles," in Roland Schaer, *Tous les savoirs du monde*, exh. cat. (Paris: Bibliothèque nationale de France/Flammarion, 1996), pp. 273–275.

73. Hans-Olof Boström, "Philipp Hainhofer als Vermittler von Luxusgütern zwischen Augsburg und Wolfenbüttel," in Jochen Brüning and Friedrich

Niewöhner, eds., *Augsburg in der Frühen Neuzeit* (Berlin: Akademie, 1995), pp. 152–154. For the larger cultural context in which such hermetic allusiveness flourished, see Thomas DaCosta Kaufmann, *Court, Cloister, and City: The Art and Culture of Central Europe, 1450–1800* (Chicago: University of Chicago Press, 1995). Also see Arthur Wheelock, *A Collector's Cabinet* (Washington, D.C.: National Gallery of Art, 1998), pp. 19–23.

74. Hans-Olof Boström, "Ein wiederentdeckter Hainhoferschrank," *Konsthistorisk Tidskrift* 64, no. 3 (1995), 143; and Boström, "Philipp Hainhofer. Seine Kunstkammer und seine Kunstschränke," in Andreas Grote, ed., *Macrocosmos in Microcosmo. Die Welt in der Stube. Zur Geschichte des Sammelns 1450 bis 1800* (Opladen: Leske + Budrich, 1994), pp. 561–563.

75. Brian J. Gibbons, "Mysticism and Mechanism: The Religious Context of George Cheyne's Representation of the Body and Its Ills," *British Journal for Eighteenth-Century Studies* 21 (Spring 1998), 10–13.

76. On the *lusus naturae*, see my *Voyage into Substance: Art, Nature, and the Illustrated Travel Account, 1760–1840* (Cambridge, Mass.: MIT Press, 1984), chap. 4: "Natural Hieroglyphics." Also see Paula Findlen, "Between Carnival and Lent: The Scientific Revolution at the Margins of Culture," *Configurations* 6 (Spring 1998), 253–256.

77. Paula Findlen, *Possessing Nature: Museums, Collecting, and Scientific Culture in Early Modern Italy* (Berkeley and Los Angeles: University of California Press, 1994), p. 201.

78. On mathematical recreations and the "games" of science, see my *Artful Science: Enlightenment Entertainment and the Eclipse of Visual Education* (Cambridge, Mass.: MIT Press, 1994), especially chaps. 1 and 2: "The Mind's Release" and "The Visible Invisible." Also see *Voyage into Substance*, chap. 2: "The Natural Masterpiece."

79. Hana Seifertova, "Der Blick in eine Gemäldegalerie—das Antwerpener Thema aus Prager Perspektive," in *Dialog mit Alten Meistern. Prager Kabinettmalerei 1690–1750*, exh. cat. (Braunschweig: Herzog Anton Ulrich-Museum, 1997), pp. 36–37.

80. For the distinction between *musée* and *musaeum*, see Paula Young Lee, "The Musaeum of Alexandria and the Formation of the *Museum* in Eighteenth-Century France," *Art Bulletin* 79 (September 1997), 385, 391.

81. Martin Pops, *Vermeer: Consciousness and the Chamber of Being* (Ann Arbor: UMI Research Press, 1984), p. 27.

82. Ivan Illich, "Guarding the Eye in the Age of Show," *Res* 23 (Autumn 1995), 47.

83. Elizabeth Legge, "Thirteen Ways of Looking at a Virgin: Francis Picabia's *La Sainte Vierge*," *Word & Image* 12 (April–June 1996), 227. See also the essay

on early twentieth-century gendering of machines by Caroline A. Jones, "The Sex of the Machine: Mechanized Bodies in Early Modernism," paper presented at the conference "Histories of Science/Histories of Art," Boston, November 4, 1995.

84. Lily E. Kay, "Cybernetics, Information, Life: The Emergence of Scriptural Representations of Heredity," *Configurations* 5 (Winter 1997), 36–39.

85. John W. Yolton, *Perception and Reality: A History from Descartes to Kant* (Ithaca: Cornell University Press, 1996), p. 22.

86. Cited in José Luis Bermúdez, Anthony Marcel, and Naomi Eilan, eds., *The Body and the Self* (Cambridge, Mass.: MIT Press, 1995), p. 153.

87. John D. Searle, "Consciousness and the Philosophers, " *New York Review* (March 6, 1997), 43–50.

88. Roger Penrose, *Shadows of the Mind: A Search for the Missing Science of Consciousness* (Oxford: Oxford University Press, 1994), p. 27.

89. See Pinker, *How the Mind Works*, p. 119.

90. Sherry Turkle, *Life on Screen: Identity in the Age of the Internet* (New York: Simon & Schuster, 1995), p. 137. On the self of the author and reader as hypertext, see George P. Landow, *Hypertext 2.0*, rev. ed. (Baltimore: Johns Hopkins University Press, 1997), pp. 90–96.

91. Umberto Eco, *The Limits of Interpretation* (Bloomington: Indiana University Press, 1995).

92. James Bailey, *After Thought: The Computer Challenge to Human Intelligence* (New York: Basic Books, 1996).

93. Michael Benedikt, ed., *Cyberspace: First Steps* (Cambridge, Mass.: MIT Press, 1991), p. 50.

94. Michael Heim, "The Erotic Ontology of Cyberspace, " in Benedikt, ed., *Cyberspace*, p. 69.

95. Baumgartner and Payn, eds., *Speaking Minds*, p. 11.

Postscript: Beyond Duality: From Adepts to Agents

1. Daniel J. Kevles and Leroy Hood, eds., *The Code of Codes: Scientific and Social Issues in the Human Genome Project* (Cambridge, Mass.: Harvard University Press, 1993), p. 380.

2. Maynard Olsen, "A Biology Lesson," lecture, Henry Gallery, Seattle, February 26, 1999.

3. Michael Heim, "The Cyberspace Dialectic," in Peter Lundenfeld, ed., *The Digital Dialectic* (Cambridge, Mass.: MIT Press, 1999), pp. 42–43.

4. Among the generally negative dialecticians of the Frankfurt School, Siegfried Kracauer stands out because of this (analogical) concern for connectiv-

ity. See Dagmar Barnouw, *Critical Realism: History, Photography, and the Work of Siegfried Kracauer* (Baltimore: Johns Hopkins University Press, 1994), p. 54.

5.   Robert E. Horn, *Visual Language: Global Communication for the 21st Century* (Bainbridge Island, Wash.: MacroVe Press, 1999).

6.   N. Katherine Hayles, "Contrasted Constructivism: Locating Scientific Inquiry in the Theater of Representation," in George Levine, ed., *Realism and Representation: Essays on the Problem of Realism in Relation to Science, Literature, and Culture* (Madison: University of Wisconsin Press, 1993), p. 39.

7.   Bruno Latour, "A Well-Articulated Primatology: Reflexions of a Fellow Traveller," in Shirley C. Strum and Linda M. Fedigan, eds., *Primate Encounters* (Chicago: University of Chicago Press, 1999), pp. 15–16.

Index

Page numbers in boldface indicate material in illustrations.